More Bestselling For D Titles by Eric Tyson

T0357367

Investing For Dummies®

A *Wall Street Journal* bestseller, this book walks you through how to build wealth in stocks, real estate, and small business as well as other investments. Also check out the recently released *Investing in Your 20s and 30s For Dummies*.

Mutual Funds For Dummies®

This best-selling guide is now updated to include current fund and portfolio recommendations. Using the practical tips and techniques, you'll design a mutual fund investment plan suited to your income, lifestyle, and risk preferences.

Personal Finance For Dummies®

Discover the best way to establish and achieve your financial goals, reduce your spending and taxes, and make wise personal financial decisions. *Wall Street Journal* bestseller with more than 1.5 million copies sold in all editions, and winner of the Benjamin Franklin business book award.

Personal Finance in Your 20s For Dummies®

This hands-on, friendly guide provides you with the targeted financial advice you need to establish firm financial footing in your 20s and to secure your finances for years to come. When it comes to protecting your financial future, starting sooner rather than later is the smartest thing you can do.

Real Estate Investing For Dummies®

Real estate is a proven wealth-building investment, but many people don't know how to go about making and managing rental property investments. Real-estate and property management expert Robert Griswold and Eric Tyson cover the gamut of property investment options, strategies, and techniques.

Small Business For Dummies®

This practical, no-nonsense guide gives expert advice on everything from generating ideas and locating start-up money to hiring the right people, balancing the books, and planning for growth. You'll get plenty of help ramping up your management skills, developing a marketing strategy, keeping your customers loyal, and much more. And, find out to use the latest technology to improve your business's performance at every level. Also available from co-authors Eric Tyson and Jim Schell, *Small Business Taxes For Dummies*.

Money Management Essentials

for **dummies**®

A Wiley Brand

Money Management Essentials

by Eric Tyson, MBA

with Bob Carlson

A Wiley Brand

Money Management Essentials For Dummies®

Published by: **John Wiley & Sons, Inc.**, 111 River Street, Hoboken, NJ 07030-5774, www.wiley.com

For general information on our other products and services, please contact our Customer Care Department within the U.S. at 877-762-2974, outside the U.S. at 317-572-3993, or fax 317-572-4002. For technical support, please visit https://hub.wiley.com/community/support/dummies.

Wiley publishes in a variety of print and electronic formats and by print-on-demand. Some material included with standard print versions of this book may not be included in e-books or in print-on-demand. If this book refers to media that is not included in the version you purchased, you may download this material at http://booksupport.wiley.com. For more information about Wiley products, visit www.wiley.com.

Library of Congress Control Number: 2025933223

ISBN 978-1-394-32606-8 (pbk); ISBN 978-1-394-32608-2 (ePDF);
ISBN 978-1-394-32607-5 (epub)

SKY10099225_030425

Contents at a Glance

Introduction.. 1

CHAPTER 1: Knowing What Financial Security Means to You.................... 3

CHAPTER 2: Establishing a Financial Safety Net.. 11

CHAPTER 3: Reducing and Repaying Debt... 27

CHAPTER 4: Protecting Yourself with Insurance....................................... 51

CHAPTER 5: Lowering Your Tax Bill 69

CHAPTER 6: Investing for the Long Haul.. 79

CHAPTER 7: Setting Financial Goals Beyond Paying Bills 101

CHAPTER 8: Estate Planning: Leaving a Legacy....................................... 113

CHAPTER 9: Staying Financially Resilient in a Volatile World 125

CHAPTER 10: Continuing Your Financial Education................................. 143

CHAPTER 11: Ten Ways to Prevent Identity Theft and Fraud 155

Index... 161

Table of Contents

INTRODUCTION 1
    About This Book 1
    Foolish Assumptions 1
    Icons Used in This Book 2
    Where to Go from Here 2

**CHAPTER 1: Knowing What Financial Security
Means to You** 3
    What Is Financial Security, and Why Should You Care? 4
        Defining what you value 4
        Assessing your current personal financial health 6
        Grasping financial lingo and trends 7
        Trying not to avoid money 8
        Dealing with insurance 9
    Making Money Decisions Amid Changing Circumstances 10

CHAPTER 2: Establishing a Financial Safety Net 11
    Preparing for Unplanned Events 11
        Building emergency reserves 12
        Navigating a personal crisis 13
    Inventorying Your Resources 15
        Surveying your accessible money and spending options 15
        Finding assistance from family 16
        Ensuring adequate insurance coverage 17
        Qualifying for societal safety nets 18
    Knowing When to Tap Your Resources 20
        Losing your job or a significant source of income 20
        Facing a medical crisis 21
        Caring for elderly parents unexpectedly 21
        Splitting from your spouse 23
        Coping with the death of a spouse 24
        Dealing with a natural disaster 25

CHAPTER 3: **Reducing and Repaying Debt**................................27

  Managing Your Feelings About the Debt You Owe....................27
    Knowing how long it will take to regain financial stability.......28
    Wise financial actions to take..29
    Boneheaded financial actions to avoid................................29
  Paying Off High-Interest Debt: A Heroic Feat............................30
    Using savings to reduce your consumer debt........................31
    Decreasing debt when you lack savings..............................33
    Turning to credit counseling agencies................................35
    Filing bankruptcy...37
  Avoiding New Debt: The Art of Saying No................................41
    Reducing your expenditures...41
    Setting and following a budget...46
    Boosting savings by reducing spending..............................48

CHAPTER 4: **Protecting Yourself with Insurance**................51

  Health Insurance (Even Superheroes Need Checkups).................51
    Mandating health insurance: The Affordable Care Act...........52
    Choosing a plan...53
    Buying health insurance..54
    Understanding subsidies...55
  Maximizing Medicare Benefits...56
    Closing Medicare's gaps..56
    Long-term care insurance..57
    Making sense of Medicare's prescription drug program.........58
  Protecting Your Income with Long-term Disability Insurance......58
    Looking at types of disability insurance coverage..................59
    Reviewing your disability insurance coverage.......................60
  Providing for Loved Ones through Life Insurance.....................61
    Term versus cash value life insurance................................62
    Figuring out how much life insurance you need....................63
  Shielding Your Assets from Unexpected Twists.........................64
    Insuring your home...64
    Insuring your car...66
    Protecting against mega-liability: Umbrella insurance............68

CHAPTER 5: **Lowering Your Tax Bill**...69

  Knowing Your Income Tax Rate...69
  Making Your Income Tax Rate Work for You............................71
    Contribute to lower your income..71
    Choose investments wisely...72

Consider capital gains 72
Strengthen your deductions.................................... 73
Trimming Employment Income Taxes 74
Contributing to retirement investment plans 74
Shifting some income... 76
Taxing Issues Regarding Children 77
Meeting Quarterly Tax Filing Requirements 78

CHAPTER 6: **Investing for the Long Haul**.............................. 79
Retirement Accounts and the Magic of Compound Interest 79
Surveying retirement account choices..................... 80
Transferring retirement accounts............................ 83
Patience and Persistence: The Tortoise Beats the
Day Trader.. 87
Making money from stocks 87
Buying stocks via mutual funds and exchange-
traded funds 88
Using hedge funds and privately managed funds.......... 90
Selecting individual stocks yourself......................... 91
Proven investment strategies................................... 92
Avoiding problematic stock-buying practices............. 93
Diversification: Not Putting All Your Eggs in One Basket 95
Spreading the wealth: Asset allocation 96
Allocating money for the long term......................... 96
Sticking with your allocations: Don't trade 98
Investing lump sums via dollar-cost averaging 98

CHAPTER 7: **Setting Financial Goals Beyond Paying Bills** 101
Dreaming of Financial Independence............................. 101
Knowing What's Most Important to You.......................... 103
Valuing retirement accounts 104
Dealing with competing goals 105
Saving for big purchases.. 106
Avoiding Over-Saving... 107
Understanding the over-saver mindset 107
Balancing spending and saving................................. 108
Keeping money accumulation in proper perspective 109
Giving yourself permission to spend more 109
Doing some retirement analysis............................... 109
Getting smart about investing your money.............. 110

Going on a news diet...110
Treating yourself to something special...........................111
Buying more gifts for the people you love 111
Going easy when it comes to everyday expenses 111

CHAPTER 8: Estate Planning: Leaving a Legacy........................113
Wills, Trusts, and Estate Planning...................................113
Starting with a will..114
Avoiding probate through living trusts 115
Considering your preparation options.....................116
Reducing estate taxes 116
Power of Attorney: Appointing Your Financial Sidekick.....117
Recognizing the importance of a POA.....................118
Choosing the right POA...119
Advanced Directives: Making Medical Decisions
Ahead of Time...120
Understanding living wills.......................................121
Signing DNRs..122
Assigning a healthcare proxy or POA 123
Authorizing HIPAA..123
Combining documents...124

**CHAPTER 9: Staying Financially Resilient in a
Volatile World**...125
Riding Economic Ups and Downs Without Losing Your Hat.....125
Examine the missteps of others 126
Avoid common mistakes...127
Embrace financial strategies that work....................128
Adopt a positive mindset 129
Adaptability: The Financial Chameleon's Superpower 129
Starting out: Your first job......................................130
Changing jobs or careers 131
Getting married...132
Buying a home 134
Having children 134
Starting a small business 137
Receiving a windfall 138
Retiring...140

CHAPTER 10: **Continuing Your Financial Education**........................143

    Identifying Reliable Sources of Financial Information 143

        Finding the best websites 144

        Checking out blogs, podcasts, and newsletters 148

        Navigating newspapers and magazines 148

        Betting on books...149

    Observing the Mass Media..150

        Alarming or informing? 150

        Teaching questionable values 151

        Worshiping prognosticating pundits 152

        Navigating social media 152

CHAPTER 11: **Ten Ways to Prevent Identity Theft and Fraud**..................155

    Save Phone Discussions for Friends Only 155

    Never Respond to Emails Soliciting Information........................156

    Review Your Monthly Financial Statements.............................156

    Secure All Receipts 157

    Close Unnecessary Credit Accounts....................................157

    Regularly Review Your Credit Reports 157

    Freeze Your Credit Reports or Place an Alert 158

    Keep Personal Info Off Your Checks 158

    Protect Your Computer and Files 159

    Safeguard Your Mail..159

INDEX...161

Introduction

Most people value financial security and independence. In this book, I help you consider what being financially secure and independent means to you. Then I show how you can manage your money to attain your personal and financial goals (most people have more than a few!).

Unfortunately, your financial well-being can be undermined by things outside of your control. Upsetting events include macro-events like the COVID-19 pandemic (2020) or financial crisis (2008), or individual life changes or personal crises, such as job loss, divorce, caring for elderly parents, and so on. Throughout this book, I share ideas that help you ride the economic roller coaster without losing your hat.

About This Book

This book provides the know-how you need to feel more confident about managing your money. It covers the essentials of sound personal financial management: living within your means, building a financial safety net, saving and investing in wise, proven investments, and securing catastrophic insurance.

You can read this book from cover to cover if you want, or you can read a particular chapter or part without having to read what comes before it. Handy cross-references direct you to other places in the book for more details on a particular subject.

Foolish Assumptions

Whenever I approach writing a book, I consider a particular audience for that book. Because of this, I must make some assumptions about who the readers are and what those readers are looking for. Here are a few assumptions I've made about you:

>> You want the best for you and yours and would like to make the most of your money. While you understand that there

are no guarantees, you'd like to best prepare your financial situation to weather a wide range of adverse conditions.

» You'd like to be able to make smarter money-management decisions when news and information hits, especially in the midst of a crisis.

» You'd like to be positioned to be able to invest at least some of your money when otherwise attractive investments have declined in value.

If any of these descriptions hits home for you, you've come to the right place.

Icons Used in This Book

The icons in this book help you find particular kinds of information that may be useful to you.

TIP

This icon points out something that can save you time, headaches, money, or all of the above!

REMEMBER

This icon flags concepts and facts that I want to ensure that you remember as you make personal finance decisions.

WARNING

With this information, I try to direct you away from blunders and mistakes that others have made when making important personal finance and related decisions.

Where to Go from Here

If you have the time and desire, I encourage you to read this book in its entirety. It provides you with the essential information you need to cultivate financial resilience in an often volatile world. You also can pick and choose the information you read based on your individual needs. Just scan the table of contents or index for the topics that interest you the most.

Chapter **1**

Knowing What Financial Security Means to You

Achieving financial independence and feeling financially secure are admittedly subjective assessments. A nest egg of $200,000 may seem like a lot to some people but not to a high-income earner who is accustomed to spending $100,000+ annually.

Now, for many people the feeling of financial security isn't simply a matter of how much money you have to your name. Numerous other factors may contribute to feeling secure financially, which I help you to understand.

In this chapter, I help you determine what financial security means to you, assess where you are now, and begin to think through how you can manage your money to accomplish your goals. I also discuss how to best position yourself to benefit from the inevitable opportunities that present themselves during tough economic times.

What Is Financial Security, and Why Should You Care?

A good place to begin is by defining what financial security means to you and what is and isn't important to you. Then I help you think through and understand where you are now and consider some fundamental aspects of managing your money that many people find challenging, such as making sense of financial trends, confronting procrastination, and dealing with insurance.

Defining what you value

If saving money is a good habit, the more you save, the better, right? Well, no, not really, unless your sole goal is to amass as much money in various accounts as possible. But what if you're not spending enough to eat a healthy diet? How about some time and money so that you can regularly rest and enjoy some recreation? What about some spending for the special people in your life?

Think about all the big decisions in your life: choosing and finding a job, a place to live, a spouse, and so on. For most people, there's a financial component to all of these. When thinking about personal goals, nearly all of them take money to accomplish. Money is inextricably linked to the rest of your life. Making the best financial decisions starts with the big picture and the rest of your life in mind — in other words, holistically.

Suppose like many people, you are working and earning money. You'd like to save and invest some of that and not have to continue working full-time for the rest of your life. But you probably have some other competing uses for your money. These may include things like saving to buy a home or start a business, expenses for your family, a future vacation, and so on.

Money shares some similarities with food. If you don't have enough, you likely notice the insufficiency of your resources. Having more than enough with some reserves and extras usually provides most people with some peace of mind. Different people, though, have different views of how much extra they may want to have.

The virtue of a capitalistic economy is that within reason, if you're willing to work hard and seek to improve yourself and your work, over time you should be able to see your money grow. The progress and advancement of technology and society generally increase the purchasing power of your money over time.

Some folks lose sight of the differences between necessities and luxuries, especially in affluent and upper-middle class communities and circles. We can always find people with bigger homes and more expensive cars who have taken more exotic vacations. The bar can continually be set higher and higher in terms of how much money we "need."

The continual improvement of products and services, particularly those that incorporate a lot of technology, leads to more folks taking for granted how "luxurious" some of today's choices are compared with those of the past. Consider what's happened with personal computers and smartphones. Today, consumers buy smartphones that have many of the same functionalities and can access far more information than personal computers could a generation or two ago. And you can buy today's smartphones for less than the cost of personal computers from a generation or two ago. Today's smartphones are like a handheld personal computer, a phone (that can easily travel with you), and a quality camera all rolled into one!

Automobiles have far more features, especially safety features like air bags and anti-lock brakes, compared to those from a generation or two ago. Today's cars are dramatically more fuel efficient, too.

Just walk through most homes and apartments today and you'll find all sorts of devices like microwave ovens, printers, HDTVs, washers and dryers, dishwashers, and so on, which are far better and relatively less costly than in prior generations. And in some cases, these devices didn't exist or weren't widespread not that many generations ago.

So, I urge you to step back and think about what it is that you value and to recognize how "luxurious" are so many of the choices and options that we have in modern American society. With many products and services, we get far more for our money than folks did a generation or two ago.

That said, we can all think of some expense categories like higher education, housing in some higher-demand cities (such as New York City and San Francisco) and portions of the healthcare industry where the rate of price increases (inflation) may exceed increases in typical wages and the general cost of living. These categories are the exception, not the rule, and you can take steps and actions to mitigate and blunt some or even much of the excessive price increases through the strategies I discuss in this book.

REMEMBER

Especially in our consumption-oriented society, some folks may get carried away with working and earning more and amassing more money. Life is short, and you can't take your money with you in the end. So, there's something to be said for balancing work, earning and saving money, and having sufficient time for family, friends, and your activities and hobbies.

Assessing your current personal financial health

What's your current personal financial health? There are numerous ways to measure that. When I've worked with clients as a financial counselor and as an educator, I've found the following exercises to be valuable:

>> **Net worth analysis:** Your ability to accomplish important financial goals, such as buying a home and someday retiring from full-time work, depends upon your net worth. To derive your net worth, you total up your financial assets and subtract your financial liabilities. I typically exclude a person's home in this analysis unless they plan to tap some portion of their home's equity, by trading down to a lower-priced property.

>> **Spending analysis:** You should know where your money goes in a typical month or year, especially if you'd like to save a greater portion of your employment income. Analyzing your historic spending can tell you just that.

>> **Saving analysis:** Over the past year, what portion of your work income were you able to save? Many people don't know the answer to that important question, and if you don't, you can't really know whether you're on track to accomplish your financial and personal goals.

>> **Your investment portfolio:** Can your investment portfolio be improved? Do you understand your current investments? How do your current holdings stack up in terms of costs/fees and performance within their respective peer groups? Do your current investment holdings match your risk and return preferences?

>> **Your home:** If you currently rent or own a home but are looking to sell and buy another, that takes some advance planning and analysis. Since housing costs can consume a significant portion of your income and budget, you should ensure that a change in your housing situation fits with your financial and personal goals and planning.

>> **Insurance review:** You should have insurance to protect you against losses that could be financially catastrophic to you and your loved ones. I know from my counseling work that many folks have gaps in their insurance coverage and are wasting money on overpriced or unnecessary policy features.

>> **Employee benefits review:** Plenty of employees don't bother to read and review their employee benefits, which typically include various insurance coverages and possibly a retirement savings plan. Employee benefits can actually be quite valuable and should be coordinated with your overall financial plan.

These elements form a personal financial plan. You can hire a competent and ethical financial planner to assemble such a plan for you, but you should beware that many folks sell products on commission or charge hefty ongoing money management fees. Others aren't interested or experienced enough to help you with nuts-and-bolts issues like analyzing your spending. This book helps you manage your money and get your personal finance house in order.

Grasping financial lingo and trends

Personal financial knowledge and literacy is an enormous obstacle for too many people, including those who have invested tremendous time, energy, and money into their formal educations. Unfortunately, such education rarely includes the essential topic of money management.

Ubiquitous gurus are another common obstacle. Everywhere you look, especially online and in the media, there are plenty of anointed experts predicting what will supposedly happen with the economy, financial markets, and all sorts of other economic variables. Listening to all these supposed experts and their often-conflicting opinions can paralyze you or make you feel that you need to hire them (or others like them) to manage your money since it appears that they know so much more than you do.

In reality, it's important that you develop a personal financial plan of action that suits your goals, needs, and concerns and doesn't involve jumping into and out of investments based upon short-term noise or news events. This is what this book can help you do.

Trying not to avoid money

One big obstacle is that just about everybody avoids dealing with some aspect of money. For some, it's as simple as avoiding looking regularly at their checking account and verifying transactions and the account balance or making decisions about where to invest saved money. Others neglect needed insurance coverage, perhaps out of fear of confronting their own mortality and vulnerabilities. Some people are plagued by broader problems such as feelings of guilt and shame about money or feeling that money seems dirty and evil.

The fact that money-related issues aren't always at the top of your priority list may well be a good sign. Perhaps you spent the past weekend with friends and family or were engrossed in a captivating book or a newly discovered streaming series. But continually avoiding money or some aspect of your finances can result in unnecessary long-term pain.

Some personal finance procrastinators can get away with their ways for a number of years. However, whether it's in the short term or the long term, eventually, problems do occur from avoiding dealing with money and related decisions, and sometimes the damage can be catastrophic.

Some money avoiders don't plan ahead and save toward future goals. Often, the reality hits home when they contact the Social Security Administration (SSA) or get an update from the SSA and discover what monthly retirement benefit amount they'll get at full retirement age (which is around age 66 to 67 for most people). The reality for many people means the realization that they'll have to continue working into their seventies in order to maintain the modest standard of living to which they've become accustomed.

Several issues typically cause a lack of retirement funds. Many money avoiders could save more money, but they typically aren't motivated and organized enough to do so. Generally, they haven't bothered to conduct even basic retirement analysis to understand how much they should be saving to reach their retirement goal (or even think about if and when they want to retire).

Because money avoiders dislike dealing with money, what they're able to save often gets ignored and languishes in low- or no-interest bank accounts. Avoiders also tend to fall prey to the worst salespeople, who push them into mediocre or poor investments with high fees. When avoiders choose their own investments, they often do so based on superficial research and analysis, which can lead to piling money into frothy investments when they're popular. Discomfort causes avoiders to bail out when things look bleak.

WARNING

Money avoiders, more often than not, lack wills and other legal documents that should specify to whom various assets shall pass and who is responsible for what (for example, administering the estate and raising minor children) in the event of their untimely demise. When money is to pass to heirs through an estate, the absence of documents can lead to major legal and family battles.

Dealing with insurance

Because insurance is an admittedly dreadful and unpalatable topic for most people, many folks avoid insurance-related issues. And while well-intentioned and commission-hungry insurance agents get some people to plug insurance gaps, these salespeople may not direct you to a policy best suited to your needs. In fact, brokers may sell you costly insurance (such as cash value life insurance) that provides them with a higher commission and you with less insurance than you need.

Insurance gaps come to light when a disability or a protracted illness occurs. Too often, we believe that these problems only happen to elderly people, but they don't. In fact, statistically, you are far more likely to miss work for an extended period of time due to a disability or lengthy illness than you are to pass away prematurely.

If others are dependent upon you financially, you likely need certain coverages that would provide for them in the event of your untimely passing, as well.

In Chapter 4, I cover the types of insurance you need to protect yourself and your assets.

Making Money Decisions Amid Changing Circumstances

When broader economic and financial crises strike, for sure bad things happen. Some people lose their jobs. Stock prices and home values generally fall. This can create opportunities for those who have cash and courage to step up and buy otherwise good investments at depressed prices.

Having a good-size cash reserve for difficult times makes sense. But how large should that reserve be? If you keep too much in cash, your investment returns will suffer. Keeping too little in cash can cause your reserves to be pinched during tough times and can leave you with little, if anything, to invest when investment prices are down.

Most people with some cash find it hard to step up and make investments while the news is filled with so much gloom. And there's the natural tendency to worry about things getting even worse. In Chapter 9, I offer insight into how you can maintain financial resilience amid changing circumstances.

Chapter **2**

Establishing a Financial Safety Net

n this chapter, I discuss how to quickly inventory and marshal your own resources when you're in the midst of a crisis and, if necessary, find someone to lean on — like a loved one you can trust — during tough times. I also inventory the government-administered social safety net programs for which you may be eligible.

I hope that your life will have far more positive events and surprises than the negative things discussed in this chapter. But I can tell you that good things come out of bad events.

Preparing for Unplanned Events

Personal crises and unplanned life changes (including happy life events) often affect your finances, so you want to manage your money for these unknowns as best you can. Establishing a financial safety net and plan before events happen can greatly ease the burden of navigating stressful situations and help ensure that you land on your feet.

TIP

Here are some general tips that apply to all types of life changes:

>> **Stay in financial shape.** An athlete is best able to withstand physical adversities during competition by prior training and eating well. Likewise, the sounder your finances are to begin with, the better you'll be able to deal with life changes

>> **Remember that changes require change.** Even if your financial house is in order, a major life change — starting a family, buying a home, starting a business, divorcing, retiring — should prompt you to review your personal financial strategies. Life changes affect your income, spending, insurance needs, and ability to take financial risk.

>> **Don't procrastinate.** With a major life change on the horizon, procrastination can be costly. You (and your family) may overspend and accumulate high-cost debts, lack proper insurance coverage, or take other unnecessary risks. Early preparation can save you from these pitfalls.

>> **Manage stress and your emotions.** Life changes often are accompanied by stress and other emotional upheavals. Don't make snap decisions during these changes. Take the time to become fully informed and recognize and acknowledge your feelings. Educating yourself is key. You may want to hire experts to help but don't abdicate decisions and responsibilities to advisors — the advisors may not have your best interests at heart or fully appreciate your needs.

Building emergency reserves

Conventional wisdom says that you should have approximately six months' worth of living expenses put away for an emergency. This particular amount may or may not be right for you, because it depends, of course, on how expensive the emergency is. Why six months, anyway? And where should you put it?

TIP

How much of an emergency stash you need depends on your situation. I recommend saving the following emergency amounts under differing circumstances (in Chapter 5, I recommend preferred places to invest this money):

>> **Three months' living expenses:** Choose this option if you have other accounts, such as a 401(k), or family members

and close friends whom you can tap for a short-term loan. This minimalist approach makes sense when you're trying to maximize investments elsewhere (for example, in retirement accounts) or you have stable sources of income (employment or otherwise).

>> **Six months' living expenses:** This amount is appropriate if you don't have other places to turn to for a loan or you have some instability in your employment situation or source of income.

>> **Up to one year's living expenses:** Set aside this much if your income fluctuates wildly from year to year or if your profession involves a high risk of job loss, finding another job can take you a long time, and you don't have other places to turn for a loan.

TIP

If your only current source of emergency funds is a high-interest credit card, first save at least three months' worth of living expenses in an accessible account before funding a retirement account or saving for other goals.

Navigating a personal crisis

This section provides a checklist of important items to keep in mind as you're navigating a personal crisis that is impacting your finances. Use this list to remind yourself of key things to do and consider when you've encountered tough times:

>> **Be prepared for tough times.** This preparation can include having an emergency reserve and flexible spending so that you can more easily reduce your spending. Try to minimize the amount of spending that you engage in that is locked in, for example, through contracts for an extended period of time.

>> **When trouble hits, set aside time to consider and discuss the situation with family or someone you can trust.** Spend time brainstorming on your topics of concern, including ways to reduce your spending.

>> **Make note of benefits you lose through an employer and develop a plan to replace needed catastrophic insurance.** You always need health insurance, and until you're financially

independent, disability insurance. If others are dependent upon your employment income, you should also have term life insurance.

» **Be flexible and keep an open mind.** A crisis can lead to opportunities for change and may include things like moving or simply changing your approach to certain aspects of your life and finances.

» **Be prepared to negotiate and advocate for yourself and situation.** This can include things like your housing and being able to meet the terms of your mortgage repayment or rental payments for a lease or dealing with an insurance company claim. If you have a hard time doing these things, enlist the support of someone who is comfortable and adept at doing this.

» **Take time for your mental health and decision making.** You should always do this, but it's especially important for you to take a little time every day to do things that you enjoy and that help you to relax. For some folks, this can be exercising, reading a good book, listening to music, and so on.

» **Understand and make use of your employee benefits.** In my work as a financial counselor, I often discovered valuable employee benefits that my clients had overlooked or forgotten they had access to.

» **Understand the tax consequences.** Many financial decisions involve tax considerations, so be sure that you understand those issues and tax reduction opportunities associated with those decisions.

» **Find out about safety nets.** When you're facing a personal financial crisis, you may qualify for some of the numerous safety net programs at the federal, state, and local levels. Please see the section "Qualifying for societal safety nets" later in this chapter for the details.

» **Make informed decisions after doing research.** When you're stressed and perhaps pressed for time with everything that's coming at you, you're more likely to make an emotionally based decision. Don't add to your difficulties by making bad decisions. Do the necessary research and consult experts or smart people who can help you to make an informed decision.

Inventorying Your Resources

You've got resources — probably more than you realize. Some will be more attractive to tap than others. This section helps you recognize, inventory, and prioritize what you have to bring to the battle.

Surveying your accessible money and spending options

First, do an inventory of your available options for quickly (or reasonably quickly) available cash. Here are the common ones that you likely have access to and how I think about their attractiveness for you to consider tapping them:

>> **Accessing your emergency reserve of cash:** I've always recommended that folks have an emergency stash of cash of at least three months' worth of living expenses and perhaps as much as six to twelve months' worth for those with more uncertainty regarding their jobs and overall situations. Saving automatically through regular contributions to savings or transfers from checking can build your emergency fund.

>> **Tapping cash value life insurance balances:** Insurance agents love to sell cash value life insurance because it pays them much higher commissions than term life insurance. If you have a cash balance in your life insurance policy, you can generally tap it by borrowing against it or by cashing in the policy. If you need life insurance, please don't do the latter until you have first secured replacement term life insurance. See Chapter 4 for more about life insurance and how to best buy it.

>> **Taking out a loan.** For most people, the quickest way to borrow money (in other words, spend money you don't have) is via a credit card. If that's the only source of funding accessible to you, be sure to shop around for a credit card with good overall terms, especially for the interest rate charged on balances carried over month-to-month. While you may be able to borrow through loans tied to other specific purchases, such as a car or furniture, when times are tough, you likely won't be in a situation where you "need" to make such purchases.

>> **Borrowing from your retirement funds.** Your retirement plan may allow borrowing. I'm generally not a fan of this approach because if you borrow this money, you will miss out on the returns on that money until your loan is repaid. If the overall economy is going through a bad period, this will likely mean missing out on a good stock market rebound, since the financial markets are forward-looking and stocks rebound well in advance of the economy actually looking better. Also, if you fail to repay a loan made against your retirement account, you will get socked with federal and state income taxes on the amount withdrawn as well as federal and state tax penalties for taking a withdrawal before age 59½.

Another option you may consider is to borrow from family, and that's the subject of the next section.

Finding assistance from family

Here are the elements or ingredients that I think generally lead to a successful lender/borrower situation between family members:

>> **Borrow from someone financially sound.** The person doing the lending should be financially well off and not harmed in a notable way in the unlikely event that the borrower ends up not being able to repay part or even all of the loan.

>> **Get it in writing.** The terms of the loan are put in writing and signed by both parties. One page may be sufficient in most cases. This step is critical to ensure that both parties are literally on the same page! Doing such an agreement leaves no ambiguity about the fact that both sides agree that it's a loan that needs to be repaid under the terms spelled out in the short agreement.

>> **Set the loan for a reasonable (in other words, not long) period of time.** Generally speaking, the shorter the time period for the loan, the better in terms of the loan being likely to be repaid. Of course, the repayment terms need to be realistic and fit within the budget of the borrower.

>> **Charge a fair interest rate.** Loans in the real world from real-world lenders charge interest. Loans between family members can certainly be done at lower interest rates than a for-profit lender would charge.

>> **Consider "what-ifs."** Your simple loan agreement should spell out things like what happens to the loan if the borrower is unable to make payments for some period of time. The loan document should also cover things like whether it's okay to pay off the loan early and what happens to the loan if something happens to the borrower.

In many cases where I have observed or heard that a family loan didn't work out or caused a rift, no loan agreement/document was in place. It's not that the document makes everything work out, but it's the process of discussing the issues and the fact that it's a loan that is expected to be repaid that helps maximize the chances that all will be good.

WARNING

A family loan can go off the rails and cause interpersonal family problems when it leads some family member(s) to feel jealous or out of favor. Sometimes family members who see other members getting a loan may perceive that as special or favored treatment that they weren't offered or didn't get. A classic situation where such feelings may arise is if parents extend a loan to one of their adult children and the other sibling(s) feel resentment. This naturally raises the idea of discussing the issue with other relevant family members before a loan is agreed to in order to minimize the potential for misunderstandings or hard feelings.

But the prospective borrower may not want everyone else in the family knowing their business or what precipitated the need for a loan from a family member. So, my suggestion is to begin with the prospective borrower to ask them how they feel about borrowing money and how others in the family may feel about it.

Ensuring adequate insurance coverage

Carrying and maintaining catastrophic insurance is essential to protect your personal financial situation and your family. You certainly don't want to lose or misuse such coverage when you're entering or in the midst of an economic downturn or personal crisis.

REMEMBER

Many folks have various insurance coverages (for example, health insurance and disability insurance) through their employers. You need to stay on top of securing needed insurance so that if you lose your job, you don't suffer any lapses in coverage. Chapter 4 provides details on what insurance you should and shouldn't carry and how and where to get the best value for your insurance dollars.

WARNING

When money is tight and times are tough, you may be tempted to cut some corners and go without needed insurance for a "short time." Please don't do that! It's impossible to predict exactly when you will need to use a particular insurance policy, so you need to maintain your coverage all the time. Don't tempt fate and risk having a major insurance claim during a period when you chose to drop a particular policy in an effort to save a little money.

Qualifying for societal safety nets

The requirements or thresholds to qualify for societal safety nets vary greatly. I find that many folks are surprised at how affluent you can be and how high your income can be to qualify for some of them. The point of this section is to explain to you the programs that are out there and get the process started for you to determine whether you may qualify for any of them.

>> **Health insurance subsidies:** When the Affordable Care Act (ACA), also known as Obamacare, was signed into law in 2010, it included subsidies for low- and moderate-income earners. The large COVID-19 relief bill known as the American Rescue Plan Act (ARP) of 2021 further expanded and increased those subsidies to include even more households that would be considered middle-class and upper-middle class. Because assets aren't an explicit factor in determining subsidies, some households that may be considered higher-income earners are also now eligible for at least partial subsidies.

   Medicare is the federal government–provided insurance for older Americans that kicks in for most people at age 65. If you are eligible for Medicare (and even if you're not currently enrolled in it), you may not sign up for a new Obamacare exchange-based plan.

   Medicaid is a state-based health insurance program that doesn't charge premiums for low-income people. You also can't sign up for an exchange-based subsidized health insurance plan if you're eligible for Medicaid in your state.

>> **Unemployment insurance benefits:** If you lose your job, you can probably collect unemployment insurance benefits while you're seeking a new job. Employers pay into unemployment insurance funds for this very reason — so that the government has funding to pay out benefits when folks lose their jobs.

The federal government, through the Department of Labor, provides federal guidelines for the state-administered unemployment benefit programs. Each state has its own eligibility guidelines for qualifying to collect unemployment benefits. These guidelines generally are based upon needing to meet a time-worked threshold or wage amount.

To find your state's unemployment information, visit: www.careeronestop.org/LocalHelp/UnemploymentBenefits/find-unemployment-benefits.aspx.

>> **Federal refundable tax credits:** There are two separate federal income tax credits — the Earned Income Tax Credit (EITC) and the Child Tax Credit (CTC) — which are designed to assist lower-income earners. Both of these tax credits include refundable portions, which means that even if you owe no federal income tax for a particular tax year (which is the case for more than 40 percent of all households), the federal government will actually pay you for a portion of the qualifying federal income tax credit. So, rather than owing or paying any federal income tax for that year, qualifying households are paid money by the federal government.

The EITC was instituted in 1975 and has been modified numerous times since. Eligibility for this tax credit is based upon family size and the amount of earned income. To see if you qualify for the EITC, you can answer a series of questions on the "EITC Assistant" at the IRS's website: https://apps.irs.gov/app/eitc.

>> **Help with housing:** Federal Housing Assistance programs are administered by the Department of Housing and Urban Development (HUD). Their most well-known and utilized program is the Housing Choice Voucher Program, which is also known as Section 8 or the Tenant Based Rental Assistance program. It is run and administered by local Public Housing Agencies (PHAs), which distribute vouchers to help pay a portion of an eligible tenant's rent. For more information about this HUD program, please visit www.hud.gov/topics/housing_choice_voucher_program_section_8. Also, HUD's Resource Locator can be found at resources.hud.gov.

TIP

U.C. Davis's Center for Poverty and Inequality Research has a compilation of the major federal safety net programs in the United States. Visit poverty.ucdavis.edu/article/war-poverty-and-todays-safety-net-0.

Knowing When to Tap Your Resources

Economies go through cycles. Good times and periods of growth and more jobs are inevitably followed by downturns and times when more people lose their jobs or face reduced salaries. In addition to crises in the broader economy or society, plenty of people are hit with a personal or household-specific crisis. In the following sections, I describe common crises that people encounter and offer recommendations for dealing with them.

Losing your job or a significant source of income

Here are my suggestions for dealing with the inevitable loss of your job someday or perhaps an unexpected reduction in income:

>> **Always be prepared to lose your job.** Unless you're incredibly fortunate or lucky or both, you will someday unexpectedly lose your job and/or face a significant reduction in your employment income.

>> **Structure your finances to afford an income dip.** Resist overspending on your housing expense. If you're really stretched buying a home with all the associated expenses, consider what you would do and how challenged you might be on a reduced income.

>> **If you lose your job, batten down the hatches.** Evaluate and slash your current level of spending as necessary. Everything should be fair game, from how much you spend on housing to how often you eat out to where you do your grocery shopping.

Avoid at all costs the temptation to maintain your level of spending by accumulating consumer debt. See Chapter 3 for more info.

WARNING

>> **Arrange to continue insurance coverage.** Most importantly, that can include insurance coverages such as health insurance and possibly disability insurance and life insurance. Replacing these on your own costs money, of course, but going without them exposes you to potentially catastrophic financial risks. See Chapter 4 for more details.

>> **Evaluate the total financial picture when relocating.** Don't call the moving company or pick your new home until

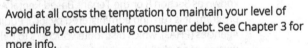

you understand the financial consequences of the different options. In addition to evaluating the salary and benefits of a given job, you also need to compare the cost of living of given locations. You'll want to pay attention to housing costs, commuting, state income and property taxes, food, utilities, and all the other major expenditure categories.

Check online for cost-of-living information and calculators such as BestPlaces.net.

Facing a medical crisis

To keep your sanity and to ensure your best health, here are some important steps to take and points to keep in mind:

>> **Check your coverage.** Make sure your health insurance coverage is being paid and in force.

>> **Take time off from your job.** If you work for an employer, they may offer sick days and/or personal days.

>> **Enlist and embrace support.** When it's your health problem, dealing with important medical decisions can feel isolating and lonely. Finding a trusted (and trustworthy) person willing and able to share some of the burden and thinking can be invaluable.

>> **Seek second opinions and do some research.** There is rarely just one clear-cut course of action to deal with a particular medical problem. Be sure that you ask any medical provider what treatment options exist for your problem and for their opinion of the pros and cons of each.

You should also do some of your own research, but please understand the dangers of unvetted things you may read online that any person with a computer can choose to publish on a website. Check and vet your sources!

Caring for elderly parents unexpectedly

Here are key issues to consider when unexpectedly needing to care for aging parents:

>> **Get involved in their healthcare.** Speak with your aging parent's primary care doctor so that you can understand their current medical condition, the need for various medications,

and how to help coordinate caregivers. Visit home-care providers and nursing homes and speak with prospective care providers.

>> **Get help where possible.** In most communities, a variety of nonprofit organizations offer information and counseling to families who care for elderly parents. Numerous for-profit agencies can help with everything from simple cleaning and cooking to health checks and medication monitoring, to assisted living and health advocacy. You may be able to find your way to such resources through your state's department of insurance, as well as through recommendations from local senior centers, doctors, and other medical providers. You'll especially want to get assistance and information if your parents need some sort of home care, nursing home care, or assisted living arrangement.

>> **Take some time off.** Caring for an aging parent, particularly one who is having health problems, can be time-consuming and emotionally draining. Do your parents and yourself a favor by using some personal or vacation time to help get things in order. Also be sure to take care of yourself and give yourself some needed downtime and a real vacation from your obligations.

>> **Understand tax breaks.** If you're financially supporting your parents, you may be eligible for a number of tax credits and deductions for elder care. Some employers' flexible benefit plans allow you to put away money on a pretax basis to pay for the care of your parents. Also explore the dependent care tax credit, which you can take on your federal income tax Form 1040. And if you provide half or more of the support costs for your parents, you may be able to claim them as dependents on your tax return.

>> **Discuss getting the estate in order.** Parents don't like thinking about their demise, and they may feel awkward discussing this issue with their adult children. But opening a dialogue between you and your folks about such issues can be healthy in many ways. Not only does discussing wills, living wills, power of attorney, living trusts, and estate planning strategies make you aware of your folks' situation, but it can also improve their plans to both their benefit and yours.

Splitting from your spouse

In most marriages that are destined to split up, both parties usually recognize early warning signs. Sometimes, however, one spouse may surprise the other with an unexpected request for divorce. Whether the divorce is planned or unexpected, here are some important considerations regarding divorce:

>> **Question the divorce.** Although some couples are indeed better off parting ways, others give up too easily, thinking that the grass is greener elsewhere, only to later discover that all lawns have weeds and crabgrass. Just as with lawns that aren't watered and fertilized, relationships can wither without nurturing. Money and disagreements over money are certainly contributing factors in marital unhappiness. Try talking things over, perhaps with a marital counselor.

>> **Separate your emotions from the financial issues.** Feelings of revenge may be common in some divorces, but they'll probably only help ensure that the attorneys get rich as you and your spouse butt heads. If you really want a divorce, work at doing it efficiently and harmoniously so you can get on with your lives and have more of your money to work with. The more spent on legal fees, the less will be left for you and your soon-to-be ex-spouse.

>> **Detail resources and priorities.** Draw up a list of all the assets and liabilities that you and your spouse have. Make sure that you list all the financial facts, including investment account records and statements. After you know the whole picture, begin to think about what is and isn't important to you financially and otherwise.

>> **Educate yourself about personal finance and legal issues.** Divorce sometimes forces non-financially oriented spouses to get a crash course in personal finance at a difficult emotional time. This book and others I've written, such as *Personal Finance For Dummies* (also published by Wiley) can help educate you financially. Peruse a bookstore and buy a good legal guide or two about divorce.

>> **Choose advisors carefully.** Odds are that you'll retain the services of one or more specialists to assist you with the myriad issues, negotiations, and concerns of your divorce.

Legal, tax, and financial advisors can help, but make sure you recognize their limitations and conflicts of interest. The more complicated things become and the more you haggle with your spouse, the more attorneys, unfortunately, benefit financially. Also, realize that you don't need an attorney to get divorced. A variety of books and kits can help you. Consider divorce by mediation. Research mediators in your area.

>> **Analyze your spending.** Some divorcees find themselves financially squeezed in the early years following a divorce because two people living together in the same property can generally do so less expensively than two people living separately. Analyzing your spending needs pre-divorce can help you adjust to a new budget and negotiate a fairer settlement with your spouse.

>> **Review needed changes to your insurance.** If you're covered under your spouse's employer's insurance plan, make sure you get this coverage replaced. If you or your children will still be financially dependent on your spouse post-divorce, make sure that the divorce agreement mandates life insurance coverage. See Chapter 4 for more about insurance. You should also revise your will.

>> **Revamp your retirement plan.** With changes to your income, expenses, assets, liabilities, and future needs, your retirement plan will surely need a post-divorce overhaul.

Coping with the death of a spouse

Of course, everyone ultimately passes away, and we all hope to live a long, healthy life and go peacefully into the night at a ripe old age. But medical problems, accidents, and other largely unpredictable events can cause an untimely death of a spouse or other important loved one. I've worked with numerous people and had other friends who have dealt with this situation, and the challenges are numerous. Here are some things to consider:

>> **Take some mental health time off.** Allow some time and space to grieve and to adjust to your new and unplanned role.

>> **Find someone to lean on.** It can be a relative, a friend, or both who can help you to cope with your new situation and be a sounding board. Just be sure that the person you're relying upon is trustworthy and without an agenda. A counselor or psychologist may be useful as well for a period of time, and some religious organizations offer very reasonably priced six- to eight-week group sessions for support and guidance. One example is mournerspath.com. Check out your faith group for offerings.

>> **Move slowly with important decisions, especially financial ones.** You may consider selling your home, moving, making changes to investments, and so on. Any of those can be a reasonable thing to do with proper time, thinking, and research. But give yourself some time to adjust and process all that has happened and changed. You also want to be sure that you aren't being pushed into making a decision by a salesperson or anyone else with a financial conflict of interest or some other agenda.

>> **Know where everything is.** In some couples, responsibility is shared for dealing with financial matters whereas with other couples, one person deals with everything. Regardless, each of you needs to know where everything (for example investment accounts, insurance policies, wills and estate documents, car titles, and so on) is located and dealt with.

Dealing with a natural disaster

Without adequate insurance (and even with insurance, in some circumstances), the financial consequences of a natural disaster can be devastating. If you're dealing with the aftermath of a natural disaster, it's too late then to do anything about the insurance you didn't have, but there are many things you can do to deal with your situation:

>> **Ensure your personal safety first.** Frontline safety responders will tell you that it's often the case that there are more fatalities in the aftermath of some natural disasters than from the disaster itself. Be careful in the aftermath of a natural disaster and don't rush out to do things that can wait or take unnecessary risks like trying to drive through a water-covered roadway.

>> **Take a hard look at your expenses.** If you're suddenly facing a period of reduced income due to a natural disaster, take a fresh look at your spending and cut non-necessities as needed. You can always restart them, and you may well find that some providers will offer you better pricing if you're set to cancel due to short-term affordability issues. Don't cut needed catastrophic insurance coverage.

>> **If you have insurance claims, be sure to document everything and be ready to negotiate and fight for what you're due.** Some insurance companies do the right thing, but too often, they will view your claim as a business expense and do what they can to minimize your payments.

Chapter **3**

Reducing and Repaying Debt

When you've suffered through tough times, it can be hard to think clearly and make thoughtful, informed decisions. To deal with a difficult situation, you may have accumulated high-interest or other "bad" consumer debt. (Some debt, such as a mortgage, can be good to have.)

In this chapter, I help you make wise decisions as you create a plan to reduce and repay any consumer debt you accumulate.

Managing Your Feelings About the Debt You Owe

At various times in your life, you'll make important financial decisions. The timing of those decisions — such as buying a home, starting or buying a small business, or contributing to a retirement savings plan — is often at your discretion. Dealing with tough times either personally or due to the broader economy can upset the timing of such decisions and how you make them.

Picking up the pieces, surveying the damage, and so on are not enjoyable expressions and topics to consider. But all of us have to do so at various times in our lives. The sooner you can grasp the reality of your situation and begin making accurate assessments, the better able you will be to make constructive decisions that will help you now and in the future.

Experiencing frustration and other negative emotions is certainly not unusual. Check your expectations when dealing with personal or economic challenges. In addition to the amount of time required to heal problems and wounds, also recognize that forward progress is fluid. While you will enjoy progress at times, you should be prepared for inevitable setbacks.

REMEMBER

Try not to dwell on the negative and things you can't change, and instead, focus on the things you *can* change. Remember the Serenity Prayer:

> God grant me the Serenity to accept the things I cannot change, Courage to change the things I can, and Wisdom to know the difference.

In this section, I want to help you acknowledge your feelings, and further, make sure that you're making good decisions and sidestepping commonly made bad ones.

Knowing how long it will take to regain financial stability

Recovery for major problematic events is usually measured in months or years, not days or weeks. For sure, you may well see tangible signs of progress over short time periods. But it's certainly not realistic to expect a major or full recovery that quickly.

Good can and often does come out of bad situations, and I certainly encourage you to be a "glass half full" kind of person with your outlook. Take major stock market declines of more than 20 percent, which are known as *bear markets*. Owning stocks during such a slide can test your nerves and optimism.

Since World War II, it has on average taken a full year for the stock market (as measured by the S&P 500 index) to recover the losses during a typical bear market. Some recent bear markets were worse — it took four years, until 2006, to recover from the

2000–2002 bear market, and it took three years, until 2012, to recover from the 2007–2009 bear market. But recover they do.

Going through a divorce, for example, is unpleasant and raises myriad financial and other issues that require your attention. But if the relationship was filled with intractable problems that continually made you miserable, moving on and forging a new life may well be the right thing to do and lead to far greater happiness. That said, there are folks who go through a divorce and find that they've still got major problems or that a new relationship sours and leads to problems similar to those in the previous failed marriage.

Wise financial actions to take

The following are some examples of generally constructive things you can do when faced with repaying a large amount of high-interest debt. In fact, you can apply these ideas to almost any circumstance that challenges your financial security:

>> **Take stock of your overall situation.** Not all debt reduction strategies apply to all situations. Before you can determine which strategies make sense for you, you must first consider your overall financial situation and assess your alternatives.

>> **Reduce discretionary spending.** Many people have some fat and waste in their spending, and cutting down on that is inevitably a good thing for your overall situation.

REMEMBER

Be sure to discuss the issue with family members, as others will surely have different priorities in mind than you do. Be patient and explain the importance and value of everyone pulling and working together, and be open to compromise.

>> **Invest more in solid investments at depressed prices.** Good things, including otherwise sound investments, sometimes go on sale. If you've planned ahead or simply accumulated some extra cash over time, a great time to deploy it would be when pessimism is in the air and investment values are down.

Boneheaded financial actions to avoid

Whether on your own or with the encouragement of outside bad advice, most often from a salesperson or someone else with a vested financial interest in your decisions, making a poor decision can add to your misery from a personal or economic crisis, especially when that crisis is compounded by the need to pay off debt. Here are some common bad ideas to sidestep:

>> **Selling investments at depressed prices:** Good investments inevitably rebound after downturns and that rebound in prices often happens quickly, so you don't want to miss out on it.

>> **Allowing important insurance policies to lapse:** Discontinuing insurance policies defeats the whole purpose of carrying catastrophic insurance coverage: that it's there when you may need it.

>> **Taking money out of retirement accounts before it's needed:** Tapping the money in your retirement accounts before you've exhausted other options is almost always a mistake due to the federal and state income tax owed as well as penalties generally applied if you're withdrawing retirement account money before age 59½.

Paying Off High-Interest Debt: A Heroic Feat

Accumulating *bad debt* (consumer debt) by buying things like new living room furniture or a new car that you really can't afford is like living on a diet of sugar and caffeine: a quick fix with little nutritional value. Borrowing on your credit card to afford an extravagant vacation is detrimental to your long-term financial health.

When you use debt for investing in your future, I call it *good debt*. Borrowing money to pay for a quality education that improves your career, to buy real estate, or to invest in a small business is like eating a well-balanced and healthy diet. That's not to say that you can't get yourself into trouble when using good debt. Just as you can gorge yourself on too much good food, you can develop financial indigestion from too much good debt or when using debt to finance poor investments or educational options.

In this section, I mainly help you battle the pervasive problem of consumer debt. You may have had good reason for accumulating these bad debts, but getting rid of them can be even more difficult than giving up the junk foods you love. In the long run, you'll be glad you did; you'll be financially healthier and emotionally happier. And after you get rid of your high-cost consumer debts, make sure you practice the best way to avoid future credit problems: *Don't borrow with bad debt.*

REMEMBER

Before you decide which debt reduction strategies make sense for you, you must first consider your overall financial situation and assess your alternatives. (I discuss strategies for reducing your current spending — which help you free up more cash to pay down your debts — in the later section "Avoiding New Debt: The Art of Saying No".)

Using savings to reduce your consumer debt

If you have the savings to pay off consumer debt, like high-interest credit card and auto loans, consider doing so. (Make sure you pay off the loans with the highest interest rates first.) Sure, you diminish your savings, but you also reduce your debts. Although your savings and investments may be earning decent returns, the interest you're paying on your consumer debts is likely higher.

WARNING

If you use your savings to pay down consumer debts, be careful to leave yourself enough of an emergency cushion. (In Chapter 2, I tell you how to determine what size emergency reserve you should have.) You want to be in a position to withstand an unexpected large expense or temporary loss of income. On the other hand, if you use savings to pay down credit card debt, you can run your credit card balances back up in a financial pinch (unless your card gets canceled), or you can turn to a family member or wealthy friend for a low-interest loan.

TIP

Here are some cash sources you may have overlooked:

>> **Borrow against your cash value life insurance policy.** If you did business with a life insurance agent, that person probably sold you a cash value policy because it pays high commissions to insurance agents. Or perhaps your parents bought one of these policies for you when you were a child. Borrow against the cash value to pay down your debts. (You

may want to consider discontinuing your cash value policy altogether and simply withdraw the cash balance.)

» **Sell investments held outside of retirement accounts.** Maybe you have some shares of stock or a Treasury bond. Consider cashing in these investments to pay down your consumer loans. Just be sure to consider the tax consequences of selling these investments. If possible, sell investments that won't generate a big tax bill.

» **Tap the equity in your home.** If you're a homeowner, you may be able to tap in to your home's *equity,* which is the difference between the property's market value and the outstanding loan balance. You can generally borrow against real estate at a lower interest rate and get a tax deduction, subject to interest deduction limitations. However, you must take care to ensure that you don't overborrow on your home and risk losing it to foreclosure.

» **Borrow against your employer's retirement account.** Check with your employer's benefits department to see whether you can borrow against your retirement account balance. The interest rate is usually reasonable. Be careful, though — if you leave or lose your job, you have to fully repay the loan by the federal income tax return due date of the following year; otherwise, the unpaid balance is treated as a taxable distribution. Also recognize that you'll miss out on investment returns on the money borrowed.

» **Lean on family.** They know you, love you, realize your shortcomings, and probably won't be as cold-hearted as some bankers. Money borrowed from family members can have strings attached, of course. Treating the obligation seriously is important. To avoid misunderstandings, write up a simple agreement listing the terms and conditions of the loan. Unless your family members are the worst bankers I know, you'll probably get a fair interest rate, and your family will have the satisfaction of helping you out. Just be sure to pay them back.

REMEMBER

Paying off consumer loans on a credit card at, say, 12 percent is like finding an investment with a guaranteed return of 12 percent — *tax-free.* You would actually need to find an investment that yielded even more — around 18 percent — to net 12 percent after paying taxes on those investment returns in order to justify not paying off your 12 percent loans. The higher your tax bracket (see Chapter 5), the higher the return you need on your investments to justify keeping high-interest consumer debt.

Even if you think that you're an investing genius and you can earn more on your investments, swallow your ego and pay down your consumer debts anyway. In order to chase that higher potential return from investments, you need to take substantial risk. You *may* earn more investing on that hot stock tip or bargain real estate, but you probably won't.

Decreasing debt when you lack savings

If you lack savings to throw at your consumer debts, and you're currently spending all your income (and more!), you need to figure out how you can decrease your spending and/or increase your income. In the meantime, you need to slow the growth of your debt by reducing the interest rate you're paying. Here are sound ways to do that:

>> **Apply for a lower-rate credit card.** If you're earning a decent income, you're not too burdened with debt, and you have a clean credit record, qualifying for lower-rate cards is relatively painless. Some persistence (and cleanup work) may be required if you have income and debt problems or nicks in your credit report. After you're approved for a new, lower-interest-rate card, you can simply transfer your outstanding balance from your higher-rate card.

CreditCards.com's website (www.creditcards.com) carries information on low-interest-rate and no-annual-fee cards (among others, including secured cards).

When you hunt around for a low-interest-rate credit card, be sure to review all the terms and conditions. Start by reading the uniform rates and terms disclosure, which details the myriad fees and conditions (especially how much your interest rate can increase for missed or late payments). Also, be sure that you understand how the future interest rate is determined on cards that charge variable interest rates.

WARNING

>> **Call the bank(s) that issued your current high-interest-rate credit card(s) and say that you want to cancel your card(s) because you found a competitor that offers no annual fee and a lower interest rate.** Your bank may choose to match the terms of the "competitor" rather than lose you as a customer. Sticking with your current card may

be better for you because canceling the credit card, especially if it's one you've had for a number of years, may lower your credit score in the short term.

>> **While you're paying down your credit card balance(s), stop making new charges on cards that have outstanding balances.** Many people don't realize that interest starts to accumulate *immediately* when they carry a balance. *You have no grace period* — the 20 or so days you normally have to pay your balance in full without incurring interest charges — if you carry a credit card balance from month to month.

Cutting up your credit cards

If you have a tendency to live beyond your means by buying on credit, get rid of the culprit — the credit card (and other consumer credit). Cut up *all* your credit cards and call the card issuers to cancel your accounts. And when you buy consumer items such as cars and furniture, do not apply for the E-Z credit.

If you can trust yourself, keep a separate credit card *only* for new purchases that you know you can absolutely pay in full each month. No one needs three, five, or ten credit cards! You can live with one (and actually none), given the wide acceptance of most cards.

Retailers such as department stores and gas stations just love to issue cards. Not only do these cards charge outrageously high interest rates, but they're also not widely accepted like Visa and Mastercard. Virtually all retailers accept Visa and Mastercard. More credit lines mean more temptation to spend what you can't afford.

If you decide to keep one widely accepted credit card instead of getting rid of them all, be careful. You may be tempted to let debt accumulate and roll over for a month or two, starting up the whole horrible process of running up your consumer debt again. Rather than keeping one credit card, consider getting a debit card.

Discovering debit cards

A *debit card* looks just like a credit card with either the Visa or Mastercard logo. The big difference between debit cards and credit cards is that, as with checks, debit-card purchase amounts are deducted electronically from your checking account within days.

(Bank ATM cards are also debit cards; however, if they lack a Visa or Mastercard logo, they're accepted by far fewer merchants.)

WARNING

If you switch to a debit card and you keep your checking account balance low and don't ordinarily balance your checkbook, you may need to start balancing it. Otherwise, you may face charges for overdrawing your account.

Here are some other differences between debit and credit cards:

>> If you pay your credit card bill in full and on time each month, your credit card gives you free use of the money you owe until it's time to pay the bill. Debit cards take the money out of your checking account almost immediately.

>> Credit cards make it easier for you to dispute charges for problematic merchandise through the issuing bank. Most banks allow you to dispute charges for up to 60 days after purchase and will credit the disputed amount to your account pending resolution. Most debit cards offer a much shorter window, typically less than one week, for making disputes.

Because moving your checking account can be a hassle, see whether your current bank offers Visa or Mastercard debit cards. If your bank doesn't offer one, shop among the major banks in your area, which are likely to offer the cards. Because such cards come with checking accounts, make sure you do some comparison shopping among the different account features and fees.

TIP

A number of investment firms offer Visa or Mastercard debit cards with their asset management accounts. Not only can these investment firm "checking accounts" help you break the credit card overspending habit, but they may also get you thinking about saving and investing your money. One drawback of these accounts is that some of them require higher minimum initial investment amounts. Among brokerages offering accounts with debit cards and competitive investment offerings and prices are Fidelity (phone 800-343-3548; website www.fidelity.com) and Schwab (phone 800-435-4000; website www.schwab.com).

Turning to credit counseling agencies

Interview any counseling agency you may be considering working with. Remember that you're the customer and you should do your homework first and be in control. Don't allow anyone or any agency to make you feel that they're in a position of power simply because of your financial troubles.

Probably the most important question to ask a counseling agency is whether it offers *debt management programs* (DMPs), whereby you're put on a repayment plan with your creditors and the agency gets a monthly fee for handling the payments. You do *not* want to work with an agency offering DMPs because of conflicts of interest. An agency can't offer objective advice about all your options for dealing with debt, including bankruptcy, if it has a financial incentive to put you on a DMP.

TIP

The Institute for Financial Literacy is a good agency that doesn't offer DMPs (phone 207-873-0068; website www.financial lit.org).

Here are some additional questions that the Federal Trade Commission suggests you ask prospective counseling agencies you may hire:

>> **What are your fees? Are there setup and/or monthly fees?** Get a specific price quote in writing.

>> **What if I can't afford to pay your fees or make contributions?** If an organization won't help you because you can't afford to pay, look elsewhere for help.

>> **Will I have a formal written agreement or contract with you?** Don't sign anything without reading it first. Make sure all verbal promises are in writing.

>> **Are you licensed to offer your services in my state?** You should work only with a licensed agency.

>> **What are the qualifications of your counselors? Are they accredited or certified by an outside organization?** If so, by whom? If not, how are they trained? Try to use an organization whose counselors are trained by a non-affiliated party.

>> **What assurance do I have that information about me (including my address, phone number, and financial information) will be kept confidential and secure?** A reputable agency can provide you with a clearly written privacy policy.

>> **How are your employees compensated? Are they paid more if I sign up for certain services, if I pay a fee, or if I make a contribution to your organization?** Employees who work on an incentive basis are less likely to have your best interests in mind than those who earn a straight salary that isn't influenced by your choices.

WARNING

Although credit counseling agencies' promotional materials and counselors aren't shy about highlighting the drawbacks to bankruptcy, counselors are reluctant to discuss the negative impact of signing up for a debt payment plan. Counselors may not want to inform you, for example, whether restructuring your credit card payments will tarnish your credit reports and scores.

Filing bankruptcy

For consumers in over their heads, the realization that their monthly income is increasingly exceeded by their bill payments is usually a traumatic one. In many cases, years can pass before people consider a drastic measure like filing bankruptcy. Both financial and emotional issues come into play in one of the most difficult and painful, yet potentially beneficial, decisions.

Understanding bankruptcy benefits

Bankruptcy allows certain types of debts to be completely eliminated or *discharged*. Debts that typically can be discharged include credit card, medical, auto, utilities, and rent.

Debts that may *not* be canceled generally include child support, alimony, student loans, taxes, and court-ordered damages (for example, drunk driving settlements).

Ideal candidates for bankruptcy have dischargeable debts (such as credit cards) and a high level of high-interest consumer debt relative to their annual income. When this ratio exceeds 25 percent, filing bankruptcy may be your best option.

REMEMBER

Eliminating your debt allows you to start working toward your financial goals. Depending on the amount of debt you have outstanding relative to your income, you may need a decade or more to pay it all off.

Coming to terms with bankruptcy drawbacks

Filing bankruptcy has a number of drawbacks. First, bankruptcy appears on your credit report for up to ten years, so you'll have difficulty obtaining credit, especially in the years immediately following your filing. However, if you already have problems on your credit report (because of late payments or a failure to pay previous debts), damage has already been done. And without savings, you're probably not going to be making major purchases (such as a home) in the next several years anyway.

TIP

If you do file bankruptcy, getting credit in the future is still possible. You may be able to obtain a *secured credit card*, which requires you to deposit money in a bank account equal to the credit limit on your credit card. Of course, you'll be better off without the temptation of any credit cards and better served with a debit card. Also, know that if you can hold down a stable job, most creditors will be willing to give you loans within a few years of your filing bankruptcy. Almost all lenders ignore bankruptcy after five to seven years.

Another drawback of bankruptcy is that it costs money, and those expenses have jumped higher due to the requirements of bankruptcy laws (more on that in a moment). I know this expense seems terribly unfair. You're already in financial trouble — that's why you're filing bankruptcy! Court filing and legal fees can easily exceed $1,500, especially in higher cost-of-living areas.

And finally, most people find that filing bankruptcy causes emotional stress. Admitting that your personal income can't keep pace with your debt obligations is painful. Although filing bankruptcy clears the decks of debt and gives you a fresh financial start, feeling a profound sense of failure (and sometimes shame) is common. Bankruptcy filers are reluctant to talk about it with others, including family and friends.

Another part of the emotional side of filing bankruptcy is that you must open your personal financial affairs to court scrutiny and court control during the several months it takes to administer a bankruptcy. A court-appointed bankruptcy trustee oversees your case and tries to recover as much of your property as possible to satisfy the *creditors* — those to whom you owe money.

If you file for bankruptcy, don't feel bad about not paying back the bank. Credit cards are one of the most profitable lines of business for banks, and the nice merchants from whom you bought the merchandise have already been paid by the bank. (*Charge-offs* — the banker's term for taking the loss on debt that you discharge through bankruptcy — are the banker's cost, which is another reason why the interest rate is so high on credit cards and why borrowing on them is a bad idea.)

Deciphering the bankruptcy laws

The Bankruptcy Abuse and Prevention Act of 2005 has a significant effect on consumers who are considering filing for bankruptcy. As you may be able to tell from the bill's name, major creditors, such as credit card companies, lobbied heavily for new laws. Although they didn't get everything they wanted, they got a lot, which — not surprisingly — doesn't benefit those folks in dire financial condition contemplating bankruptcy. Don't despair, though; help and information can overcome the worst provisions of this law. Here are the major elements of the personal bankruptcy laws:

>> **Required counseling:** Before filing for bankruptcy, individuals must complete credit counseling, the purpose of which is to explore your options for dealing with debt, including (but not limited to) bankruptcy and developing a debt repayment plan.

Historically, many supposed "counseling" agencies have provided highly biased advice. Be sure to read the earlier section "Turning to credit counseling agencies" to find out what conflicts of interest agencies have and to get advice on how to pick a top-notch agency.

To have debts discharged through bankruptcy, the new law requires a second type of counseling called "Debtor Education." All credit counseling and debtor education must be completed by an approved organization on the U.S. Trustee's website (www.justice.gov/ust). Click on the link Credit Counseling & Debtor Education (www.justice.gov/ust/credit-counseling-debtor-education-information).

>> **Means testing:** Some high-income earners may be precluded from filing the form of bankruptcy that actually discharges debts (called Chapter 7) and instead be forced

to use the form of bankruptcy that involves a repayment plan (called Chapter 13).

Recognizing that folks living in higher cost-of-living areas tend to have higher incomes, the law allows for differences in income by making adjustments based upon your state of residence and family size. The expense side of the equation is considered as well, and allowances are determined by county and metropolitan area. I won't bore you with the details and required calculations here. Few potential filers are affected by this provision. For more information, click on the Means Testing Information section (www.justice.gov/ust/means-testing) on the U.S. Trustee's website (www.justice.gov/ust).

>> **Increased requirements placed on filers and attorneys:** The means testing alone has created a good deal of additional work for bankruptcy filers, work generally done by attorneys. Filers, including lawyers, must also attest to the accuracy of submitted information, which has attorneys doing more verification work. Thus, it's no surprise that when the new bankruptcy laws were passed, legal fees increased significantly — jumps of 30 to 40 percent were common.

>> **New rules for people who recently moved:** Individual states have their own provisions for how much personal property and home equity you can keep. Prior to the passage of the current laws, in some cases, shortly before filing bankruptcy, people actually moved to a state that allowed them to keep more. Under the new law, you must live in the state for at least two years before filing bankruptcy in that state and using that state's personal property exemptions. To use a given state's *homestead exemption,* which dictates how much home equity you may protect, you must have lived in that state and owned a home for at least 40 months.

Choosing between Chapter 7 and Chapter 13

You can file one of two forms of personal bankruptcy: Chapter 7 or Chapter 13. Here are the essentials regarding each type:

>> **Chapter 7 bankruptcy allows you to discharge, or cancel, certain debts.** This form of bankruptcy makes the most sense when you have significant debts that you're legally

allowed to cancel. (See "Understanding bankruptcy benefits" earlier in this chapter for details on which debts can be canceled, or discharged.)

>> **Chapter 13 bankruptcy comes up with a repayment schedule that requires you to pay your debts over several years.** Chapter 13 stays on your credit record (just like Chapter 7), *but it doesn't eliminate debt,* so its value is limited — usually to dealing with debts like taxes that can't be discharged through bankruptcy. Chapter 13 can keep creditors at bay until you work out a repayment schedule in the courts.

Avoiding New Debt: The Art of Saying No

The vast majority of people in America have some "unnecessary" (in other words, luxury) spending in their budget. Even if you believe that all the money you spend is for necessities, there are probably some ways for you to reduce your spending on the various goods and services you purchase. If you can reduce your spending by just 5 percent, you can make enormous progress toward accomplishing your longer-term personal and financial goals.

In this section, I present you with a smorgasbord of ways to reduce your spending and boost your saving. I also explain some useful ways for you to budget going forward.

Reducing your expenditures

It's one thing to want to reduce your spending and quite another to actually do it. Sloppiness in our spending more typically happens when times are good and money is more plentiful.

Whenever you make a purchase (of a product or service), it pays to shop around and make sure that you're getting value for your money. Remember that you don't always get what you pay for. Sometimes less-costly items are better.

Also, don't assume that reducing your spending has to entail great sacrifices. Often, simple changes in behavior can go a long way toward reducing your spending. For example, buying things in bulk typically reduces the cost per item purchased.

Other ways to reduce spending are more challenging. Keep in mind that what you're willing and able to reduce will be different from what your neighbor is able to do. The following sections highlight proven ways to trim spending and boost your savings. You can cherry-pick those that you are more interested in trying.

Housing expenses

For most people, the money that they spend on shelter is their single largest expenditure (or second biggest behind taxes). In addition to your monthly mortgage payment, property taxes, and homeowner's insurance, other home-related expenses include maintenance of the home, commuting costs, and educational and other expenses for your children given the amenities and services of the community.

There are various strategies to reduce your homeownership expenses:

>> **Spend less on a home.** What do you do if you already own a home that is stretching your finances thin? Many people think of their housing expenses as fixed. It's not true in the vast majority of cases. After weighing the costs of selling and buying, you may want to consider a move to a less-expensive area or residence.

>> **Keep an eye on interest rates.** If they fall at least 1 percent from the level at which you bought, consider the costs and benefits of refinancing.

>> **Check on property value.** If property prices in your area have been falling, you may be able to appeal to lower your property's assessed value and reduce your property taxes.

>> **Consider a renter.** In the spirit of brainstorming ideas, perhaps you can stay in your current home but find ways to bring in some rental income to help offset some of your costs. You can take in a longer-term renter, for example. This may be more palatable if your home has a self-contained area/unit for the renter.

REMEMBER

If you are currently a renter, you might move to a less-expensive rental or move into a shared rental. Living alone certainly has its advantages, but it is expensive. Also, consider eventually buying a property. It may seem counterintuitive but being a renter can be quite expensive. Think long term: As a property owner,

someday your mortgage will eventually be paid off. In the meantime, a fixed-rate mortgage payment doesn't increase over the
years. Your rent, on the other hand, does generally increase with
the cost of living or inflation.

Trimming other expenses

Here are expenses other than those related to housing you may
be able to trim:

>> **Taxes:** For most people, taxes are typically their second
largest expense category after housing. Reducing your taxes
generally requires some advance planning. Making sound
financial decisions involves considering tax and other
financial ramifications. Don't wait until you're ready to file
your tax return to find out how to reduce your tax burden.
Please see Chapter 5 for strategies to lower your taxes.

>> **Retirement account contributions:** When you're going
through unusually tough times and need to find ways to
improve your cash flow, you may consider cutting back on
these contributions if necessary.

I far prefer finding other ways to reduce real "spending" and
only reducing retirement account contributions as a last
resort. History has strongly shown that continually investing
in stocks during a general economic downturn ends up
being a rewarding move as it often leads to making purchases at attractive reduced prices.

If you do weigh reducing these contributions, consider the
immediate tax impact if you were funding accounts that
provided an up-front tax break. In other words, recognize
the fact that you won't "save" the full amount of the reduced
contributions. You'll just see an increased cash flow equal to
the after-tax value of the reduced contributions. Also, I highly
recommend trying to contribute enough to employer plans
to gain the matching dollars for which you're eligible.

>> **Food and dining:** Eating in restaurants is costly, particularly
if you're not careful about where and what you eat. When
you do eat out, to keep costs down, minimize the alcohol
and desserts, which can greatly increase the cost of a meal
and undermine its nutritional value. Also try going out more
for lunch rather than dinner, which is usually more expensive. Or even better, learn to cook at home.

Regarding groceries, try to keep a decent inventory of things at home (but don't go overboard with perishables, which you may end up tossing out if you don't use them in time). This will minimize trips to the store and the need to dine out for lack of options at home. Try to do most of your shopping through discount warehouse-type stores, which offer low prices for buying in bulk, or grocery stores that offer bulk purchases or discount prices. If you live alone, don't be deterred — find a friend to share the large purchases with you.

>> **Cars and transportation:** When you buy a car, research what the car is worth. The dealer markup, especially on new cars, can be substantial. Numerous publications and services such as Consumer Reports (www.consumerreports.org), Kelley Blue Book (www.kbb.com), and Edmunds (www.edmunds.com) provide this information. Before you purchase, also consider insurance costs of the different makes and models you're considering. Before committing to buy a particular make and model, call auto insurers to shop for insurance quotes, as rates vary greatly and should factor into your purchase decision.

Avoid taking an auto loan or lease. The seemingly reasonable monthly payment amount of loans and leases deludes people into spending more on a car than they can really afford. In the long term, paying with cash is less costly.

TIP

If you owe on an auto loan, consider selling that car if you can manage without it. Getting out of an auto lease before its official end is more challenging. Two websites — www.swapalease.com and www.leasetrader.com — help match folks looking to exit a lease early with people interested in taking over a lease. You can also contact local dealers to see if they'd be interested in buying the car from you.

TIP

Also take a hard look at whether you need a car. Although living in a particular community may appear to save you money, it may not if it requires you to have a car because of the lack of other transportation options such as public transit or the distance from work.

>> **Recreation and entertainment:** Think of ways to substitute activities to reduce spending without reducing your enjoyment. Exchange invitations with friends to cook dinner at home rather than going out to restaurants. Don't be shy about using coupons or special offers at restaurants you

normally frequent. Find friends to visit when you travel. Attend a matinee movie instead of one during the high-priced evening hours. Many of the most enjoyable things in life — time spent with family and friends, outdoor activities, and so on — don't have to cost much or even any money at all.

>> **Clothing:** Avoid the temptation to buy new clothes for a new season or to use shopping as a hobby. If you enjoy the visual stimulation, go window shopping and leave all forms of payment at home. (Carrying a small amount of cash is fine!) Avoid fashions that are trendy and that you won't wear after the trend moves on. Minimize clothing that requires dry cleaning, which is costly and exposes your body to unneces-sary and unhealthy chemicals.

TIP

If you have recently purchased costly new clothing for which you now have buyer's remorse, consider returning it for a refund. Seek a cash refund, not a future credit/gift certificate to be used only at that merchant.

If you have old clothing that you absolutely refuse to wear anymore, donate it to a charity such as Goodwill or the Salvation Army. Ask for a receipt and take a write-off on your tax return if you itemize. Alternatively, consider listing for sale some of your valuable and lesser-worn clothing at a consignment store or at an online resale site.

>> **Utility bills:** Check out opportunities to make your home more energy efficient. Adding insulation and weather-stripping, installing water-saving devices, and reducing use of electrical appliances can pay for themselves in short order. Many utility companies will even do a free energy review or audit of your home and suggest money-saving ideas.

TIP

You may qualify for Residential Energy Credits, which reduce your tax bill (see IRS Form 5695). Also check out the state-specific energy tax credits you may be eligible for by visiting the website "Database of State Incentives for Renewables & Efficiency" at www.dsireusa.org.

>> **Insurance:** Insurance fills a vital and useful role. You don't want to be in the position of absorbing a financial catastro-phe. That's why, for example, you want adequate homeown-er's and health insurance. Beyond essential coverage, there's no need to waste money on insurance. Many people overspend on insurance by purchasing coverage that's

unnecessary or that covers small potential losses (such as when shipping a $100 or $200 item). To read about essential insurance coverages you may need, see Chapter 4.

Take high deductibles on your insurance policies — as much as you can afford in the event of a loss. If you are no longer dependent on your employment income and have sufficient financial resources to retire, there's no need to continue paying for disability insurance.

Also, be sure to shop around. Rates vary significantly among insurers. Of course, an insurer's quality of service and financial stability are important as well.

>> **Kid-related expenses:** Child care is often a major expense for parents of young kids. For some people, this is a necessity; for others, this is a choice. Check that your analysis of what you earn from your work and what you spend on child care makes sense.

Share with your children the realities of your family's finances and set limits on purchases and activities — this will help them to find out about financial responsibility and obligations and why you can't purchase every item advertised on TV.

>> **Charitable contributions:** Your charitable contributions are part of your budget, and as such, should be reviewed. Did you know that Americans are among the most giving people on Earth? Can you afford the amount that you are contributing? Perhaps you're at a stage of life where you should give less. The decision is yours — just give it some extra consideration!

Setting and following a budget

Some people budget for the same reason that businesses do — so that the difference between the amount of money coming in and going out is not left to chance. Suppose that you analyze your past six months' worth of spending and realize that you're saving just 5 percent of your income. Perhaps you set as a goal saving 10 percent of your income. How do you accomplish that? You can go through the various spending categories and set targets that cut your spending enough so that your rate of savings increases to 10 percent. That's what budgeting is all about.

Budgeting is not perfect, and it offers no guarantees. All a budget represents is a plan or set of targets. You may plan to cut your spending on streaming services and delivered food in half, but whether or not you do it in actuality is another matter. Don't let temptation get the better of you!

There are two common ways to develop a budget. The first method involves examining each of your spending categories that I discuss in the "Reducing your expenditures" section earlier in this chapter and developing your best estimate for how much to reduce in each. Most people will cut more in some categories than others. You must decide which expenditures provide you with the most value. It involves trade-offs, and it is rarely easy.

The other method of budgeting is to start from scratch. Rather than looking at changes to your existing spending, you figure out how much you would like to be spending in the different categories. You start with a clean slate so to speak — you're not constrained by starting with or examining what you're currently spending. The advantage of this approach is that it allows for a more significant change. The disadvantage is that the estimates can be unrealistic and harder for you to achieve.

Almost everything is fair game for change in the long haul. In the short term, some expenses are easier to reduce than others. People who have difficulty saving money tend to think of everything in their budget as a necessity. The reality is that there are opportunities to spend less on many items that seem like necessities or are things we spend money on mostly out of habit.

Develop a plan and check back periodically to see how you're doing. You may go over a little in one category, but you may be able to make up for it by staying under budget in another.

Part of smart spending and budgeting involves keeping an emergency cushion for unexpected expenses. What if you lose your job or your roof springs a leak? What if both of these unfortunate events happen soon? How would you stay afloat?

Ideally, you should have an emergency reserve of at least three months' worth of living expenses in an account that is liquid and accessible without penalty. The riskier and more volatile your employment income is, the greater the reserve you should have. If your job is unstable and you have no family members to turn to for financial help, you may want to keep as much as a year's worth of money in your emergency reserve.

Boosting savings by reducing spending

Here are the common traits among those who are able to consistently save a healthy portion of their income. Successful savers

>> **Understand needs versus wants.** Don't define necessities by what those around you have. A new $30,000 car is not a necessity, although some people try to argue that it is by saying, "I need a way to get to work." Transportation, in this case for work, is a necessity, not a new $30,000 car! What about a good-quality used car? What about carpooling, public transportation, or living close enough to work to be able to walk or bike most days? I'm not going to tell anyone exactly how they should spend their money. But I will tell you that if you take out an auto loan to buy a car that you really can't afford, and you take a similar approach with other consumer items you don't truly need, you're going to have great difficulty saving money and accomplishing your goals and will probably feel stressed.

>> **Routinely question spending and value research.** Prior to going shopping for necessities that aren't everyday purchases, make a list of the items you're looking for and do some research first. (*Consumer Reports* is a useful resource.) After you're sure that you want an item; your research has helped you identify brands, models, and so on that are good values; and you've checked in with your bank or money market account to ensure that you can afford it, check in with various retailers and compare prices. When you set out to make a purchase, only buy what's on your list.

WARNING

The internet can be a time-efficient tool for performing research and price comparisons, but be careful of common online problems. The first is advertising that masquerades as informative articles. The second problem is small online retailers who may be here today and gone tomorrow or who may be unresponsive after the purchase. Finally, internet retailers are adept at pushing additional items that they have good reason to believe will appeal to you given your other purchases.

» **Always look for the best values for products purchased.**
Value means the level of quality given the price paid for the
item. Don't assume that a more expensive product is better,
because you often don't get what you pay for. That said, you
can sometimes get a significantly better-quality product by
paying a modest amount more. Don't waste money on
brand names. If you're like most folks, you've bought
products for the status you thought they conveyed or
because you simply assumed that a given brand-name
product was superior to the alternative choices — without
thoroughly researching the issue before making the
purchase. But thanks to advertising costs, brand-name
products are frequently more expensive than less well-
known brands of comparable quality.

» **Reduce time spent on earning and spending money.**
The saddest part about being on the work and consumption
treadmill is how much of your time and life you may occupy
earning and then spending money. Consider in a typical
week how many hours you spend working and shopping.
In addition to the time actually spent at work, consider
commute time and time spent getting dressed and prepared
for work. Now add in all the time you spent shopping and
buying things. Compare the grand total of time spent on
work- and shopping-related activities to time spent on the
things you really enjoy in life.

» **Make saving money a habit.** Just as with changing what
you eat or your exercise routine (or lack thereof), modifying
your spending and savings habits is easier said than done.

IN THIS CHAPTER

» Finding affordable health insurance

» Getting the most from your
Medicare benefits

» Figuring out disability coverage

» Comparing term versus cash value
life insurance

» Protecting your assets (home, auto, and
excess liability insurance)

Chapter **4**

Protecting Yourself with Insurance

I n this chapter, I discuss the importance of protecting your future income from disability, death, or large unexpected medical expenses. I also discuss the insurance coverage you should seek for any major assets that you've acquired: your home, your car, and your personal property.

Health Insurance (Even Superheroes Need Checkups)

Before Medicare (the government-run insurance program for the elderly, covered in the later section, "Maximizing Your Medicare Benefits") kicks in at age 65+, odds are that you'll obtain your health insurance through your employer. Be thankful if you do. Employer-provided coverage eliminates the headache of having to shop for coverage, and it's usually cheaper than coverage you buy on your own.

Whether you have options through your employer or you have to hunt for a plan on your own, the following sections cover the major issues to consider when selecting among the health insurance offerings in the marketplace.

Mandating health insurance: The Affordable Care Act

The Patient Protection and Affordable Care Act (also referred to as Obamacare) and the Health Care and Education Reconciliation Act enacted comprehensive healthcare reform in the United States.

Now, employer group health plans are subject to these rules:

>> Plans offering dependent coverage must offer coverage to adult children up to age 26. The coverage isn't taxable to the employee or dependent.

>> Plans must provide preventive care without cost-sharing and must cover certain child preventive care services as recommended by the government. This rule applies only to new group health plans.

>> Employers must offer coverage that meets government requirements to full-time employees or make nondeductible payments to the government.

>> Plans must remove all annual dollar limits on participants' benefit payments. They may not impose lifetime limits.

>> Plans must limit cost-sharing and deductibles to levels that don't exceed those applicable to a health-savings-account-eligible, high-deductible health plan.

>> Plans must remove all preexisting condition exclusions on all participants.

>> Plans may not have waiting periods of longer than 90 days.

Higher-income taxpayers are now hit with higher tax rates on their investments, as well as higher Medicare tax rates to help pay for Obamacare. Taxpayers with total taxable income above $200,000 (for a single return) or $250,000 (for a joint return) from any source are subject to a 3.8 percent tax on the *lesser* of the following:

>> Their net investment income (for example, interest, dividends, and capital gains)

>> The amount, if any, by which their modified adjusted gross income exceeds the dollar thresholds

Taxpayers with earned income above $200,000 (for a single return) or $250,000 (for a joint return) are subject to an additional 0.9 percent Medicare tax (in other words, rising from 1.45 percent to 2.35 percent) on wages in excess of those amounts. Employers aren't required to match the payment of this incremental increase, which is applicable only to the employee.

Choosing a plan

Here are some important points to consider when choosing a health insurance plan:

>> **Major medical coverage:** You need a plan that covers the *big* potential expenses: hospitalization, physician, and ancillary charges, such as X-rays and laboratory work. If you're a woman and you think that you may want to have children, make sure that your plan has maternity benefits.

>> **Choice of healthcare providers:** Plans that allow you to use any healthcare provider you want are becoming less common and more expensive in most areas. Health maintenance organizations (HMOs) and preferred provider organizations (PPOs) are the main plans that restrict your choices. They keep costs down because they negotiate lower rates with selected providers.

HMOs and PPOs are more similar than they are different. The main difference is that PPOs still pay the majority of your expenses if you use a provider outside their approved list. If you use a provider outside the approved list with an HMO, you typically aren't covered at all.

TIP

If you have your heart set on particular physicians or hospitals, find out which health insurance plans they accept as payment. Ask yourself whether the extra cost of an open-choice plan is worth being able to use their services if they're not part of a restricted-choice plan. Also be aware that some plans allow you to go outside their network of providers as long as you pay a bigger portion of the incurred medical costs. If you're interested in being able to use alternative types of providers, such as acupuncturists, find out whether the plans you're considering cover these services.

» **Lifetime maximum benefits:** The Affordable Care Act has generally required health plans to do away with *lifetime maximums* (the maximum total benefits a plan will pay over the course of time you're insured by the plan). If you're shopping for a noncompliant plan, ideally choose a plan that has no maximum or that has a maximum of at least $5 million.

» **Deductibles and co-payments:** To reduce your health insurance premiums, choose a plan with the highest deductible and co-payment you can afford. As with other insurance policies, the more you're willing to share in the payment of your claims, the less you have to pay in premiums. Most policies have annual deductible options (such as $250, $500, $1,000, and so on) as well as co-payment options, which are typically 20 percent or so.

When choosing a co-payment percentage, don't let your imagination run wild and unnecessarily scare you. A 20 percent co-payment doesn't mean that you have to come up with $20,000 for a $100,000 claim. Insurance plans generally set a maximum out-of-pocket limit on your annual co-payments (such as $1,000, $2,000, and so on); the insurer covers 100 percent of any medical expenses that go over that cap.

TIP

For insurance provided by your employer, consider plans with low out-of-pocket expenses if you know you have health problems. Because you're part of a group, the insurer won't increase your individual rates just because you're filing more claims.

Most HMO plans don't have deductible and co-payment options. Most just charge a set amount — such as $25 — for a physician's office visit.

» **Guaranteed renewability:** The Affordable Care Act generally requires health insurers to continue your plan coverage regardless of any changes in your health. You want a health insurance plan that keeps renewing your coverage without you having to prove continued good health. If good health could be guaranteed, you wouldn't need health insurance in the first place.

Buying health insurance

Due to the Affordable Care Act (Obamacare), the way Americans buy and pay for health insurance is going through some upheaval. In addition to traditional insurance agents, numerous states operate health insurance exchanges that offer health plans that comply with the Affordable Care Act. To see if your state offers a health insurance exchange, visit www.healthcare.gov/marketplace-in-your-state/. If you live in a state without its own exchange, you can enroll in one at www.healthcare.gov.

You can buy many health plans through agents, and you can also buy some directly from the insurer. When health insurance is sold both ways, buying through an agent usually doesn't cost more.

If you're self-employed or you work for a small employer that doesn't offer health insurance as a benefit, get proposals from the larger and older health insurers in your area. Larger plans can negotiate better rates from providers, and older plans are more likely to be here tomorrow.

Many insurers operate in a bunch of different insurance businesses. You want those that are the biggest in the health insurance arena and are committed to that business. Nationally, Blue Cross, Blue Shield, Kaiser Permanente, Aetna, UnitedHealth, CIGNA, Assurant, and Anthem are among the older and bigger health insurers.

Also check with professional or other associations that you belong to, because plans offered by these groups sometimes offer decent benefits at a competitive price due to the purchasing-power clout that they possess. A competent independent insurance agent who specializes in health insurance can help you find insurers who are willing to offer you coverage.

Health insurance agents have a conflict of interest that's common to all financial salespeople working on commission: The higher the premium plan they sell you, the bigger the commission they earn. So an agent may try to steer you into higher-cost plans and avoid suggesting some of the strategies I discuss in the preceding section for reducing your cost of coverage. (Good agents can help guide you to the best plans that cover preexisting conditions and offer the lowest costs for your medications. Be sure to provide them with this information and compare options carefully.)

Understanding subsidies

Though the bad news is that many people faced much higher-priced policies due to the ACA, the good news is that some of those folks may qualify for government subsidies that help reduce the effective price of said policies. (Of course, this money doesn't come out of thin air; it comes from the federal government and therefore taxpayers.)

Qualifying for a subsidy depends on your family income and how many children you have. Subsidies are available to qualified individuals and families whose incomes fall in the range of 100 percent to 400 percent of the poverty line (assuming they buy a policy on a government exchange). At the top of the spectrum for 2025, an individual making just under $60,240 would be eligible for a subsidy, as would a family of four earning less than $124,800. To be eligible for a subsidy, you may not have access to health insurance coverage through an employer (including a family member's employer) and not be eligible for coverage through Medicare, Medicaid, the Children's Health Insurance Program (CHIP), or other forms of public assistance. The income thresholds vary based upon zip code — check out the handy subsidy calculator at www.kff.org/interactive/subsidy-calculator/.

TIP

If you're self-employed and end up receiving subsidies, be careful to keep track of your earnings. If you end up making more than you thought you would in a given year, you can end up having to pay back part of your subsidy. Of course, the reverse is also true: If you make less than expected, you may receive a refund.

Maximizing Medicare Benefits

Medicare, the government-run health insurance plan for those age 65 and over, is a multi-part major medical plan. Enrollment in Part A (hospital expenses) is automatic. Part B, which covers physician expenses and other charges, including home healthcare coverage; Part C, supplemental Medicare coverage (sold through private insurers); and Part D, for prescription drugs (provided through private insurers) are optional. Supplemental insurance policies, also known as Medigap coverage, may be of interest to you if you want help paying for the costs that Medicare doesn't pay.

Closing Medicare's gaps

Medigap coverage generally pays the deductibles and co-payments that Medicare charges. For the first 60 days of hospitalization, you pay $1,600 total out of your own pocket. If you have an unusually long hospital stay, you pay $400 per day for the 61st through the 90th day, $800 per day for the 91st through the 150th day, and all costs beyond 150 days. Clearly, if you stay in a hospital for many months, your out-of-pocket expenses can escalate; however, the longest hospitalizations tend not to last for many months. Also note that Medicare's hospitalization benefits refresh when you're out of the hospital for 60 consecutive days.

If you're unable to pay for the deductibles and co-payments because your income is low, making a long hospital stay a financial catastrophe for you, *Medicaid* (the state-run medical insurance program for low-income people) may help pay your bills. Alternatively, Medigap insurance can help close the gap.

TIP

Check with your physician(s) to see whether they charge a fee higher than the one listed on Medicare's fee schedule. If your physician does charge a higher fee, you may want to consider going to another physician if you can't afford the fee or if you want to save some money. (But don't drop your current doctor before finding another who accepts Medicare and you as a patient. Some doctors are not accepting Medicare patients.)

Long-term care insurance

The biggest reason that elderly people consider long-term care insurance is that Medicare pays only for the first 100 days in a skilled nursing facility. Anything over that is your responsibility. Unfortunately, Medigap policies don't address this issue, either.

Insurance agents who are eager to earn a hefty commission will often tell you that long-term care (LTC) insurance is the solution to your concerns about an extended stay in a nursing home. Don't get your hopes up. Policies are complicated and filled with all sorts of exclusions and limitations. On top of all that, they're expensive.

The decision to purchase LTC insurance is a trade-off. Do you want to pay thousands of dollars annually, beginning at age 60, to guard against the possibility of a long-term stay in a nursing home (or possibly to pay for in-home assistance if you qualify)? If you live into or past your mid-80s, you can end up paying $100,000+ on an LTC policy (not to mention the lost investment earnings on these insurance premiums).

Consider buying LTC insurance if you want to retain and protect your assets and it gives you peace of mind to know that a long-term nursing home stay is covered. But do some comparison shopping, and make sure that you buy a policy that pays benefits for the long term. A year's worth (or even a few years' worth) of benefits won't protect your assets if your stay lasts longer.

TIP

Be sure to get an LTC policy that adjusts the daily benefit amount for increases in the cost of living. Get a policy that covers care in your home or other settings if you don't need to be in a high-cost nursing home, and make sure that it doesn't require prior hospitalization for benefits to kick in. To keep premiums down, also consider a longer exclusion or waiting period — three to six months or a year before coverage starts.

Making sense of Medicare's prescription drug program

As if there weren't enough confusing government programs, Uncle Sam created yet another that began in 2006 — the Medicare (Part D) prescription drug plan. Although Medicare supplement plans typically include prescription coverage, traditional Medicare does not. With traditional Medicare, you need to purchase a separate Part D plan.

Visit www.medicare.gov for helpful information on drug plans and how to select one. For example, click on the Formulary (drug) Finder to identify specific insurer plans that cover your current medications or your anticipated future medications.

AARP's website, www.aarp.org, also has plenty of information and resources to find out more about these confusing plans.

Protecting Your Income with Long-term Disability Insurance

During your working years, your future income-earning ability is likely your most valuable asset — far more valuable than a car or even your home. Your ability to produce income should be protected, or insured.

Even if you don't have dependents, you probably need disability coverage. Are you dependent upon your income? Long-term disability (LTD) insurance replaces a portion of your lost income in the event a disability prevents you from working.

Nearly everyone should carry LTD during their working years. One exception: You're already financially independent/wealthy and no longer need to work for the income but do so anyway.

REMEMBER

You generally can't predict when and what type of disability you may suffer. That's because many disabilities are caused by medical problems (such as arthritis, cerebral palsy, diabetes, glaucoma, multiple sclerosis, muscular dystrophy, stroke, and so on) and accidents (such as head injuries, spinal injury, loss of limb or amputation, and so on).

Looking at types of disability insurance coverage

Generally speaking, you should have long-term disability insurance that provides a benefit of approximately 60 percent of your gross (pretax) income. Since disability benefit payments are tax-free if you pay the premium, they should replace your current after-tax earnings.

You may be an exception to the guideline if you have significant assets and are close to being financially independent or you earn a high income and spend far less than that. In both such cases, you may want to buy only enough coverage to replace a more modest portion of your current income.

TIP

If you're just getting started in a field (for example, starting a new business or beginning work at an entry level in a professional service field) and you expect your income to be significantly higher in future years, there's another option to consider. You can obtain a policy that enables you to buy a higher level of benefits ("future increase/purchase option") in the future without a health exam, or you can simply shop for a larger policy down the road.

State disability insurance programs and the Social Security Disability Insurance program do not generally provide adequate disability coverage for the long term. State programs typically only pay benefits for up to a maximum of one year, which isn't going to cut it if you truly suffer a long-term disability that can last many years. While one year of coverage is better than none, the premiums for such short-term coverage often are higher per dollar of benefit than those available through the best private insurer programs.

Although the Social Security program pays long-term benefits, you will receive payments only if you are not able to perform any substantial, gainful activity for more than a year or if your disability will result in death. In fact, most applicants for Social Security disability benefits coverage are turned down. Furthermore, Social Security disability payments are only intended to provide for basic subsistence living expenses.

Worker's compensation, if you have coverage through your employer, will not pay benefits at all if you get injured or become sick away from your job. Such narrow coverage that only pays benefits under a limited set of circumstances is not the comprehensive insurance you need.

Reviewing your disability insurance coverage

Features of a disability policy that are worth having include the following:

>> **Definition of disability:** Disability should be defined in such a way that the policy guarantees you benefits if you cannot perform your regular occupation. If you work as a teacher, for example, your disability policy shouldn't require you to take a job as a cashier.

>> **Noncancelable and guaranteed renewable:** These terms guarantee that your policy cannot be canceled because of poor health conditions. If you purchase a policy that requires periodic physical exams, you can lose your coverage when you are most likely to need it.

>> **Insurer's financial health:** The insurance company should have strong financial health with the leading credit-rating agencies.

>> **Benefit period:** You need a policy that would pay you benefits until an age at which you would become financially

self-sufficient. For most people, that would require obtaining a policy that pays benefits to age 65 or 67 (when Social Security retirement benefits begin). If you are close to being financially independent and expect to accomplish that or retire before your mid-60s, seek a policy that pays benefits for five years.

» **Waiting period:** This is the "deductible" on disability insurance, which is the time between your disability and when you begin collecting benefits. As with other types of insurance, take the highest deductible (in other words, the longest waiting period) that your financial circumstances allow. The minimum allowable waiting period on most policies is 30 days and the maximum can be up to one to two years. Most people should consider a waiting period of at least 90 or 180 days.

» **Residual benefits:** This option pays you a partial benefit if you have a disability that prevents you from working full time.

» **Cost-of-living adjustments:** This feature automatically increases your benefit payment once you are disabled by a set percentage or in step with inflation.

To get disability insurance proposals, start by considering any professional associations for your occupation or profession. If that's not an option, interview some good agents in your area who specialize in disability insurance.

Providing for Loved Ones through Life Insurance

If you have dependents, you may also need life insurance. Ask yourself and your family how they would fare if you died and they no longer had your income. If your family is dependent upon your income and you would want them to maintain their current standard of living in your absence, and they would not be able to do so with your passing, you need life insurance.

Term versus cash value life insurance

Despite the variety of names that life insurance marketing departments have cooked up for policies, life insurance comes in two basic flavors:

>> **Term insurance:** This insurance is pure life insurance. You pay an annual premium for which you receive a particular amount of life insurance coverage. If you, the insured person, pass away, your beneficiaries collect; otherwise, the premium is gone, but you're grateful to be alive!

>> **Cash value insurance:** All other life insurance policies (whole, universal, variable, and so on) combine life insurance with a supposed savings feature. Not only do your premiums pay for life insurance, but some of your dollars are also credited to an account that grows in value over time, assuming you keep paying your premiums. On the surface, this type of insurance sounds potentially attractive. People don't like to feel that their premium dollars are getting tossed away.

WARNING

Cash value insurance has a big catch. For the same amount of coverage (for example, for $100,000 of life insurance benefits), cash value policies cost you about eight times (800 percent) more than comparable term policies.

Insurance salespeople know the buttons to push to interest you in buying the wrong kind of life insurance. I'm going to tell you how you can save hours of time and thousands of dollars. Ready? *Buy term life insurance.*

Cash value life insurance should only be considered by folks with a high enough net worth that they anticipate having an estate planning "problem." When you buy a cash value policy and place it in an irrevocable life insurance trust, the death benefits can pass to your heirs free of federal estate taxes.

Under current tax law, you can leave up to $11.7 million free of federal estate taxes to your heirs (for tax year 2021). If you're married, you can pass on double these amounts through the use of a bypass trust. So, most people don't have an estate planning "problem." Therefore, one might think that the vast majority of people buy term insurance, not cash value policy. Surprisingly, 40 percent of all life insurance policies sold are cash value, and only 60 percent are term policies.

Given the needs and level of affluence of the broad insurance-buying public, 99+ percent of the policies sold should be term! Few people need and would most benefit from cash value policies. The fact that many people are being sold the wrong type of policy is again highlighted by the fact that the average cash value policy sold is for only $85,000 in coverage. Clearly, these policies aren't being bought by wealthy folks but instead are being peddled to many middle-class people.

Figuring out how much life insurance you need

Consider that the amount of life insurance you should buy should be determined based upon how many years' worth of your income you seek to replace. For example, if you have young children and desire to replace your income over the next 20 years, you multiply your after-tax annual income by about 15. (See Figure 4-1 for the multipliers to use for varying numbers of years.) So, if your after-tax income is $40,000 yearly, you should buy a $600,000 term life policy.

---

1. Your annual after-tax employment income $_____
   (Look at last year's tax return or Form W-2.)

2. To replace your income for this many years, multiply by: _____
   5 years × 5
   10 years × 9
   15 years × 12
   20 years × 15
   25 years × 17
   30 years × 19

3. Multiply line 1 by line 2 _____

FIGURE 4-1: Insurance needs worksheet.

If you've determined you need some life insurance because you have financial dependents and you're not yet financially independent, remember that your goal here is adequate income protection in the event of the death of an income provider. Life insurance should not be viewed as an investment vehicle!

Use the worksheet in Figure 4-1 to determine how much term life insurance to purchase.

This analysis assumes that your beneficiaries invest the life insurance proceeds and earn a modest annual rate of return of about 6 percent, while inflation runs at about 3 percent per year.

TIP

If you bought a term life policy many years ago or you didn't really shop around, get quotes now. You may be able to save a lot on the cost of your coverage by switching carriers.

A good place to obtain term life insurance proposals is a quotation service such as AccuQuote (www.accuquote.com; 800-442-9899) or ReliaQuote (www.reliaquote.com; 800-940-3002). Also check out USAA (www.usaa.com; 800-531-8722).

Shielding Your Assets from Unexpected Twists

If your home burns to the ground, a comprehensive homeowner's insurance policy should pay for the cost of rebuilding the home. Similarly, you need to protect your auto and shield yourself from excess liabilities. In this section, I describe the essential insurance coverage you need to protect these important assets.

REMEMBER

Managing your money effectively means protecting yourself from financial losses. You should buy insurance to protect your home and auto for two reasons:

>> **Your assets are valuable.** If you were to suffer a loss, replacing the assets with money out of your own pocket can be a financial catastrophe.

>> **A lawsuit can drain your finances.** Should someone be injured or killed in your home or because of your car, a lawsuit can be financially devastating.

Insuring your home

This section explains what you need on a home insurance policy and what you don't and how to get the best value for your money. I walk you through the elements of a homeowner's insurance policy — get out yours if you own a home.

TIP

If you're renting, you may want to obtain a renter's policy for two major reasons. First, is to protect your personal property, and second, is for some liability protection.

Here are the major elements on a homeowner's policy:

>> **Dwelling:** Your home insurer should determine approximately how much it would cost (based on size and cost per square foot) to rebuild your home should it be a total loss. Make sure that your policy comes with "guaranteed replacement cost" coverage. This makes the insurer pay for the full cost to rebuild your home should it cost more than the dwelling coverage portion of your policy. Please note, though, that different insurers define their guarantees differently. Most place some sort of a cap on the coverage — for example, at 20 or 30 percent above the dwelling coverage on your policy.

>> **Other structures:** This covers separate structures such as a shed, fencing, or a free-standing garage. If this coverage is higher than necessary given the structures on your land, ask the insurer about options to reduce this coverage amount.

>> **Personal property:** This portion of the policy covers the contents of your home: furniture, clothing, personal possessions, and so on. The coverage amount is typically derived as a portion (for example, three-quarters) of the dwelling portion of your policy. A good policy will cover the full cost to replace damaged items — be sure this is what you're paying for or inquire about the cost of a rider to provide this benefit. Some insurers will allow you to reduce your coverage amount from their standard level if you feel that would adequately insure your personal property.

>> **Loss of use:** This again is standard coverage and often a portion (for example, 20 percent) of the dwelling coverage. If you can't reasonably live in your home after it is damaged, this part of your policy will pay for you to rent and enjoy a similar standard of living.

>> **Personal liability:** If someone sues you for an accident relating to your home, this portion of the policy kicks in. As with your auto insurance, you should have enough liability to protect at least twice your assets. For coverage greater than $500,000, you would typically get excess liability coverage in

a separate policy (see the later section "Protecting against mega-liability: Umbrella insurance").

>> **Medical payments to others:** This is standard on most policies and provides limited coverage for out-of-pocket costs for accidents on your property.

Sometimes the location you want or need to live in comes with the added risk of certain disasters happening. Be sure to get catastrophic coverage as needed in your area. When considering a given home, be sure to investigate the risk of flooding, hurricanes, earthquakes, and landslides.

TIP

If possible, buy a home at low risk for natural disasters. An excellent warning sign for high-risk property is if you have difficulty finding insurance and find only overly expensive coverage from one or two companies.

Prospective real estate buyers can also research environmental hazards and issues of a specific property they may buy. Environmental Data Resources produces an EDR Neighborhood Environmental Report, which costs $100. You can order a report through an "EDR certified" home inspector, but you need not order a home inspection from that inspector. Call 800-352-0050 or visit EDR's website at www.edrnet.com.

Insuring your car

If your car is involved in an accident, auto insurance helps pay for the damage to the cars and property involved. It can also help pay for associated medical expenses. This section talks about what you should have and probably don't need on your auto insurance policies.

Locate a copy of your most recent auto insurance statement. Often called a *declaration*, this statement should detail your coverage types and amounts, and premiums (cost).

The following list goes through each of the elements of your policy:

>> **Liability:** Auto accidents can harm other people and damage property, and for accidents in which you're at fault, you can be sued. The liability portion of your policy provides coverage for these claims and comes in varying amounts; for example, $15,000, $30,000, $50,000, $100,000, $300,000, and

so on. This coverage amount is per accident. You should have liability coverage of at least two times the value of your assets. If you have significant assets, you can more cost-effectively pick up additional liability protection after $300,000 or $500,000 of liability coverage on your auto policy through an umbrella or excess liability policy (see the later section "Protecting against mega-liability: Umbrella insurance").

» **Medical payments:** This optional rider generally provides $5,000 or $10,000 in medical benefits to you or other passengers in your car for medical expenses not covered by their health insurance policy. This coverage is considered nonessential because it is capped at a relatively small amount, and if someone lacks health insurance, $5,000 or $10,000 in benefits won't cover much. If you're at fault and you're sued, your liability coverage will protect you and help pay for the medical expenses of the other party if you're deemed at fault.

» **Uninsured motorist:** This coverage allows you (and your vehicle's passengers) to be compensated for pain and suffering, lost wages, and out-of-pocket medical expenses when you're in an accident with an uninsured or underin-sured motorist. Think of this coverage as buying liability coverage for the other party if they don't have sufficient coverage. Once you have adequate health and disability insurance that would take care of lost wages and medical expenses in an accident, being able to collect for pain and suffering isn't really necessary.

» **Collision:** This provides reimbursement for damage done to your car in an accident. As with other types of insurance that you purchase, take the highest deductible (such as $500 or $1,000) you can comfortably live with. The deductible represents the amount of money that you must pay out of your own pocket if you have a loss for which you file a claim. A high deductible helps keep down the cost of your coverage and eliminates the hassle of filing small claims.

» **Other than collision:** Sometimes known as comprehensive coverage, this provides insurance for damage done to your car for things other than accidents. For example, if you're driving down the road and a rock skips off the road and cracks your windshield, or your car that is parked on the street is damaged by someone driving by or parking near you, this coverage will pay for damage after your deductible.

As with collision coverage, to reduce your premiums, choose as high a deductible (such as $500 or $1,000) as you are comfortable with.

>> **Other riders:** Other typical add-ons that insurers and agents may put on your policy include towing, rental car reimbursement, and so on. Skip these because they ultimately cover small potential dollar items and aren't worth insuring for. Spend your insurance money on protecting against the big potential losses.

Protecting against mega-liability: Umbrella insurance

Umbrella insurance (which is also referred to as *excess liability insurance*) is liability insurance that's added on top of the liability protection on your home and car(s). If, for example, you have $700,000 in assets, you can buy a $1 million umbrella liability policy to add to the $300,000 liability insurance that you have on your home and car. Expect to pay a couple hundred dollars — a small cost for big protection. Each year, thousands of people suffer lawsuits of more than $1 million related to their cars and homes.

Umbrella insurance is generally sold in increments of $1 million. So how do you decide how much you need if you have a lot of assets? You should have at least enough liability insurance to protect your assets, and preferably enough to cover twice the value of those assets. To purchase umbrella insurance, start by contacting your existing homeowner's or auto insurance company.

Chapter **5**

Lowering Your Tax Bill

F ederal, state, and local income taxes take a large bite out of most people's income. So, you must remember to consider taxes in the process of budgeting and planning your financial future.

Knowing Your Income Tax Rate

Your taxes are not fixed. There's no reason that you can't utilize some simple and legal strategies to reduce your tax burden. First, it helps to know what your current income tax rate is — most people don't.

REMEMBER

Income taxes have a major impact on most major financial decisions such as investing, retirement planning, and real-estate purchases. If you make these sorts of financial decisions without understanding and factoring in taxes, you're probably paying a lot more in taxes than you need to be. Understanding the tax implications may also cause you to take a different course of action.

You pay income taxes on what's known as your *taxable income*. This is simply the sum of your income, including that from employment and investments, minus your allowable deductions.

If you pull out your tax return from last year or track your tax payments (check your payroll records and quarterly tax filings with the IRS), you can quickly figure the total income taxes that you paid in a given year. Although it's enlightening to know the total income taxes you paid, this number alone won't help you make better financial decisions.

REMEMBER

A more useful tax number to know, which people are less likely to recognize, is their *marginal income tax rate*. This is the rate of income tax that you are paying on your last dollars of income. Many people don't realize that the income tax system is structured such that you pay a lower rate of tax on your first dollars of income.

As your earnings increase, you pay higher rates of tax on your income but only on your income above certain threshold amounts. These brackets are transparent to you throughout the year because you pay tax at a steady rate based on your total expected income for the year.

As you're considering your marginal income tax rate, count both federal and state income taxes. You can find the most recent federal and state income tax brackets at https://taxfoundation.org. (Click the Data tab, and for the Data Area, choose Federal or State.) Table 5-1 shows the 2025 federal tax rates for singles and married households filing jointly. Tax rates vary by state, so be sure to check the tax rate in your state.

TABLE 5-1 ## 2025 Federal Income Tax Brackets and Rates

Tax Rate	For Single Filers	For Married Individuals Filing Joint Returns
10%	$0 to $11,925	$0 to $23,850
12%	$11,925 to $48,475	$23,850 to $96,950
22%	$48,475 to $103,350	$96,950 to $206,700
24%	$103,350 to $197,300	$206,700 to $394,600
32%	$197,300 to $250,525	$394,600 to $501,050
35%	$250,525 to $626,350	$501,050 to $751,600
37%	$626,350 or more	$751,600 or more

Making Your Income Tax Rate Work for You

Knowing your marginal income tax rate allows you to assess the tax impact of various financial decisions. You pay income taxes when you earn income from employment or from most investments held outside retirement accounts, and you pay sales tax when you purchase many goods. The simplest and most powerful way to reduce the tax bite in your budget is to spend less (which saves you money on sales taxes) and invest what you save in a tax-advantaged way.

Contribute to lower your income

The single best way for most wage earners to reduce their taxable income is to contribute to retirement accounts, such as 401(k), 403(b), and SEP-IRA accounts. Contributions to these accounts are generally free of federal and state income tax. Thus, in the year of the contribution, you save on federal and state income taxes. Taxes are owed when you withdraw the money, probably in retirement. Therefore, the prime advantage of these accounts is that, over many years, you get to hold onto and invest money that would otherwise have gone to taxes when you originally earned the money.

You may also benefit if, like most people, you are in a lower income bracket in retirement. Even if your tax bracket doesn't decrease in your golden years, retirement accounts should still save you on taxes. (See Chapter 6.)

Two simple but important prerequisites prevent many people from taking advantage of this terrific tax break. First, you need to spend less than you earn so that you can "afford" to fund your retirement account(s). You certainly don't want to contribute to retirement accounts if you are accumulating debt on a credit card, for example. Plenty of people need to reduce their spending before being able to take advantage of a retirement savings plan.

The second obstacle to funding a retirement account is having access to one. Some employers don't offer retirement savings plans. If yours doesn't, lobby the benefits department and consider other employers who offer this valuable benefit. If you're self-employed, you may establish your own plan — typically an SEP-IRA.

Choose investments wisely

Whenever you invest money outside a retirement account, you should weigh the potential tax consequences. Income produced from your investments is exposed to income taxation. In matters of financial health, remember that it matters not what you make but what you get to keep after taxes.

Suppose you are considering two investments. The first is a traditional bank savings account that is paying, say, 2 percent. Another alternative you are considering is a tax-free money market fund. Although this investment option pays less — 1.6 percent — this return is federal and state tax-free. Which investment should you choose?

The answer depends on your tax bracket. The savings account pays 2 percent, but this interest is fully taxable. If, between federal and state income taxes, you pay 30 percent, then you don't get to keep the 2 percent interest. After paying taxes, you'll end up with just 1.4 percent.

Now compare this 1.4 percent after-tax rate of interest to the 1.6 percent tax-free money market fund yield. The tax-free money market fund provides you with more to keep. If you are in a low tax bracket, however, the savings account can be a better deal.

In addition to savings and money market accounts, bonds also come in tax-free and taxable interest versions. If you're in a higher tax bracket, tax-free bonds may be preferable.

Consider capital gains

Another issue to consider when investing nonretirement money is capital gains taxes. If you sell an investment held outside a retirement account at a higher price than what you purchased it for, you will owe tax on the profit, known as a *capital gain*. The tax rates for capital gains work a bit differently than on regular income.

Long-term capital gains — that is, for investments held for at least one year — are taxed at a maximum 20 percent by the IRS (high-income earners may be subject to an additional 3.8 percent investment surtax from Obamacare legislation). Losses from selling securities at a loss may be used to offset gains so long as the offsetting gains and losses are from investments for the long term.

Short-term capital gains (which can be offset by short-term losses) on investments held less than one year are taxed at your ordinary income tax rates.

All things being equal, it's best to avoid investments and trading practices that produce much in capital gains, especially short-term. Among mutual funds, for example, some funds, particularly those that engage in a lot of trading, tend to produce greater capital gains.

Strengthen your deductions

In addition to reducing the amount of your taxable income, maximizing your deductions legally also trims your tax bill. Here are some viable methods to consider:

» **Check to see whether you can itemize.** If you haven't been itemizing deductions on your tax return (which you do using the *Schedule A* form), examine the deductions, subject to limitations, that you can claim to itemize. These include state and local income taxes, real-estate mortgage interest and property taxes, and charitable contributions (including out-of-pocket expenses and mileage costs). The only way to know if you can take a larger deduction by itemizing is to total them up and compare the total to the so-called standard deduction.

» **Consider shifting and bunching deductions.** If you have nearly enough deductions in a year, you may consider grouping together, or bunching, more of your deductions into one year. Suppose you expect to have more itemized deductions next year since interest rates are rising and you will be paying greater interest on your adjustable-rate mortgage. Rather than contributing money to your favorite charities in December of this year, you might wait until January in order to qualify for itemizing in the next tax year.

» **Convert consumer debt into tax-deductible debt.** Interest on debt on credit cards and auto loans is not tax-deductible. Mortgage interest debt for your home, on the other hand, is generally tax-deductible up to $750,000 of indebtedness (the limit is $1 million if your mortgage was originated before

December 16, 2017, or for a home you had under a binding contract that was in effect before December 16, 2017, as long as the home purchase closed before April 1, 2018). If you have sufficient equity in your home, you may be able to borrow against that equity and gain a tax deduction to boot. Just be careful not to get into the habit of continually raiding your home's equity — remember, all that debt has to be paid back. Cut up those credit cards after paying off their balances with the home's equity.

>> **Own real estate.** For a home you live in, mortgage interest is largely deductible as explained in the previous bullet. Property taxes are deductible expenses that you may claim on Schedule A up to $10,000 per year when combined with your state income taxes. These deductions serve to effectively lower the long-term cost of owning real estate. Investment real estate has far broader deductions.

>> **Check out Schedule C.** If you're self-employed, make sure to find out about completing Schedule C, "Profit or Loss from Business," and the many legal deductions you may take on that form. Check out the latest edition of my *Small Business Taxes For Dummies* (Wiley).

Trimming Employment Income Taxes

You're supposed to pay taxes on income you earn from work. Countless illegal methods can reduce your taxable employment income — for example, not reporting it — but if you use them, you can very well end up paying a heap of penalties and extra interest charges on top of the taxes you owe. And you may even get tossed in jail. Because I don't want you to serve jail time or lose even more money by paying unnecessary penalties and interest, this section focuses on the best *legal* ways to reduce your income taxes on your earnings from work.

Contributing to retirement investment plans

A retirement investment plan is one of the few relatively painless and authorized ways to reduce your taxable employment income. Besides reducing your taxes, retirement plans help you build up a nest egg so you don't have to work for the rest of your life.

You can exclude money from your taxable income by tucking it away in employer-based retirement plans, such as 401(k) or 403(b) accounts, or self-employed retirement plans, such as SEP-IRAs. If your combined federal and state marginal tax rate is, say, 33 percent and you contribute $1,000 to one of these plans, you reduce your federal and state taxes by $330. Do you like the sound of that? How about this: Contribute another $1,000, and your taxes drop *another* $330 (as long as you're still in the same marginal tax rate). And when your money is inside a retirement account, it can compound and grow without taxation.

WARNING

Many people miss this great opportunity to reduce their taxes because they *spend* all (or too much) of their current employment income and, therefore, have nothing (or little) left to put into a retirement account. If you're in this predicament, you first need to reduce your spending before you can contribute money to a retirement plan. (Chapter 3 explains how to decrease your spending.)

If your employer doesn't offer the option of saving money through a retirement plan, lobby the benefits and human resources departments. If they resist, you may want to add this to your list of reasons for considering another employer. Many employers offer this valuable benefit, but some don't. Some company decision-makers either don't understand the value of these accounts or feel that they're too costly to set up and administer.

If your employer doesn't offer a retirement savings plan, individual retirement account (IRA) contributions may or may not be tax-deductible, depending on your circumstances. You should first maximize contributions to the previously mentioned tax-deductible accounts.

TIP

Lower- and moderate-income earners can gain a federal tax credit known as the "Saver's Credit." Married couples filing jointly with adjusted gross incomes (AGIs) of less than $79,000 and single taxpayers with an AGI of less than $39,500 can earn a tax credit (claimed on Form 8880) for retirement account contributions. Unlike a deduction, a *tax credit* directly reduces your tax bill by the amount of the credit. This credit, which is detailed in Table 5-2, is a percentage of the first $2,000 contributed (or $4,000 on a joint return). The credit is not available to those under the age of 18, full-time students, or people who are claimed as dependents on someone else's tax return.

TABLE 5-2 **Special Tax Credit for Retirement Plan Contributions**

Singles Adjusted Gross Income	Married-Filing-Jointly Adjusted Gross Income	Tax Credit for Retirement Account Contributions
$0–$23,750	$0–$47,500	50%
$23,750–$25,500	$47,500–$51,000	20%
$25,500–$39,500	$51,000–$79,000	10%

REMEMBER

One good reason not to fund a retirement account is having a specific goal, such as saving to purchase a home or start a business, that necessitates having access to your money. Not funding a retirement account may make sense in two other atypical situations:

» **You're temporarily in a low tax bracket.** This circumstance can come about if, for example, you lose your job for an extended period of time or are in school. In these cases, you're unlikely to have lots of spare money to contribute to a retirement account anyway! If you have some employment income, consider the Roth IRA.

» **You have too much money socked away already.** If you have a large net worth inside retirement accounts as you approach your later years, continuing to fund your retirement may be counterproductive. You will eventually be forced to make annual withdrawals (required minimum distributions) from these accounts, which can push you into higher and higher tax brackets in your retirement years if you have significant sums stashed in retirement accounts.

Shifting some income

Income shifting, which has nothing to do with money laundering, is a more esoteric tax-reduction technique that's an option only to those who can control *when* they receive their income.

For example, suppose your employer tells you in late December that you're eligible for a bonus. You're offered the option to receive your bonus in either December or January. If you're pretty certain that you'll be in a higher tax bracket next year, you should choose to receive your bonus in December.

Or, suppose you run your own business and you think that you'll be in a lower tax bracket next year. Perhaps you plan to take time off to be with a newborn or take an extended trip. You can send out some invoices later in the year so your customers won't pay you until January, which falls in the next tax year.

Taxing Issues Regarding Children

You surely have enough challenges raising kids today without the headache of dealing with the IRS. The good news is that dealing with taxes for your children need not be complicated.

REMEMBER

Your first tax encounter with the IRS as a family is securing a Social Security number for your child. Your child must have a Social Security number by age 1 for you to claim the child as a dependent on your tax return. Form SS-5, "Application for a Social Security Card," is available online at www.ssa.gov/forms/ss-5.pdf or by calling the Social Security Administration at 800-772-1213.

The IRS allows you a couple of different ways to defray child care costs with tax breaks. First, through your employer's benefits plan, you may be able to set aside money on a pretax basis to pay for child care expenses. This not only saves you on federal income tax, but also on Social Security and Medicare tax and also generally on state income tax.

You may come out ahead taking the "dependent care tax credit" instead. Each parent must work at least on a part-time basis (unless a spouse is disabled or a full-time student) in order to be eligible for the credit, and the children must be under the age of 13. (Exceptions are allowed if your child is physically or mentally handicapped.) Complete IRS Form 2441 to claim this credit.

Meeting Quarterly Tax Filing Requirements

When you work for a company, your employer withholds money from your paycheck and sends income tax payments on your behalf to the IRS and your state. If you are self-employed or earn income in retirement or from other investments, you are responsible for paying estimated taxes to the IRS and your state on a quarterly basis.

For making and estimating your quarterly federal income tax payments, you can obtain IRS Form 1040-ES at www.irs.gov/pub/irs-pdf/f1040es.pdf or by calling the IRS (800-829-3676) and asking for it.

If you run your own company, note that you are required to withhold and send in taxes from your employees' paychecks. This may include federal, state, and local taxes, including those for Social Security and unemployment insurance. IRS Forms 940 and 941 provide more details about these rules and regulations. Alternatively, for a modest fee, you can hire one of the numerous payroll processing firms with good reputations.

Chapter **6**

Investing for the Long Haul

Most working folks need to make their money work hard in order for it to grow fast enough to provide the financial security they need for the long haul. Meeting this need involves taking some risk; you have no way around it.

In this chapter, I explain how retirement accounts and other investment options work, and how you can create a strategy to get the most out of your options.

Retirement Accounts and the Magic of Compound Interest

To take advantage of retirement savings plans and the tax savings that accompany them, you must spend less than you earn. Only then can you afford to contribute to these retirement savings plans, unless you already happen to have a stash of cash from previous savings or an inheritance.

Luckily, if you have 15 to 20 years or more before you need to draw on the bulk of your retirement account assets, time is on your side. As long as the value of your investments has time to recover, what's the big deal if some of your investments drop a bit over a year or two? The more years you have before you plan to retire, the greater your ability to take risk.

The common mistake that many younger adults make is neglecting to take advantage of retirement accounts because of their enthusiasm for spending or investing in nonretirement accounts. Not investing in tax-sheltered retirement accounts can cost you hundreds, perhaps thousands, of dollars per year in lost tax savings. Add that loss up over the many years that you work and save, and not taking advantage of these tax reduction accounts can easily cost you tens of thousands to hundreds of thousands of dollars in the long term.

The sooner you start to save, the less painful it is each year to save enough to reach your goals, because your contributions have more years to compound. Each decade you delay saving approximately doubles the percentage of your earnings that you need to save to meet your goals. If saving 5 percent per year in your early 20s gets you to your retirement goal, waiting until your 30s to start may mean socking away approximately 10 percent to reach that same goal; waiting until your 40s means saving 20 percent. Start saving and investing now!

TIP

Think of your retirement accounts as part of your overall plan to generate retirement income. Then allocate different types of investments between your tax-deferred retirement accounts and other taxable investment accounts to get the maximum benefit of tax deferral.

Surveying retirement account choices

A *retirement account* is simply a shell or shield that keeps the federal, state, and local governments from taxing your investment earnings each year. You choose which investments you want to hold inside your retirement account shell.

If you earn employment income (or receive alimony), you have options for putting money away in a retirement account that compounds without taxation until you withdraw the money. In most cases, your contributions to these retirement accounts are tax-deductible.

The following sections describe the types of retirement accounts that are suited to various situations.

Company-based retirement plans

Larger for-profit companies generally offer their employees a 401(k) plan, which typically allows saving up to $23,500 per year (for tax year 2025). Many nonprofit organizations offer their employees similar plans, known as 403(b) plans. Contributions to both traditional 401(k) and 403(b) plans are deductible on both your federal and state taxes in the year that you make them. Employees of nonprofit organizations can generally contribute up to 20 percent or $23,500 of their salaries, whichever is less.

There's a benefit in addition to the up-front and ongoing tax benefits of these retirement savings plans: Some employers match your contributions. (If you're an employee in a small business, you can establish your own SEP-IRA.) Of course, the challenge for many people is to reduce their spending enough to be able to sock away these kinds of contributions.

Some employers are offering a Roth 401(k) account, which, like a Roth IRA (discussed in the next section), offers employees the ability to contribute on an after-tax basis. Withdrawals from such accounts generally aren't taxed in retirement.

If you're self-employed, you can establish your own retirement savings plans for yourself and any employees you have. *Simplified Employee Pension-Individual Retirement Accounts* (SEP-IRA) allow you to put away up to 20 percent of your self-employment income up to an annual maximum of $70,000 (for tax year 2025).

Individual Retirement Accounts

If you work for a company that doesn't offer a retirement savings plan, or if you've exhausted contributions to your company's plan, consider an *Individual Retirement Account* (IRA). Anyone who earns employment income or receives alimony may contribute up to $7,000 annually to an IRA (or the amount of your employment income or alimony income, if it's less than $7,000 in a year). A nonworking spouse may contribute up to $7,000 annually to a spousal IRA.

Your contributions to an IRA may or may not be tax-deductible. For tax year 2025, if you're single and your adjusted gross income is $79,000 or less for the year, you can deduct your full IRA contribution. If you're married and you file your taxes jointly, you're entitled to a full IRA deduction if your AGI is $126,000 per year or less.

TIP

If you can't deduct your contribution to a standard IRA account, consider making a contribution to a nondeductible IRA account called the *Roth IRA*. Single taxpayers with an AGI less than $150,000 and joint filers with an AGI less than $236,000 can contribute up to $7,000 per year to a Roth IRA. Although the contribution isn't deductible, earnings inside the account are shielded from taxes, and unlike withdrawals from a standard IRA, qualified withdrawals from a Roth IRA account are free from income tax.

TIP

Should you be earning a high enough income that you can't fund a Roth IRA, there's an indirect "backdoor" way to fund a Roth IRA. First, you contribute to a regular IRA as a nondeductible contribution. Then, you can convert your regular IRA contribution into a Roth IRA. Please note that this so-called backdoor method generally only makes sense if you don't have other money already invested in a regular IRA because in that case, you can't simply withdraw your most recent contribution and not owe any tax.

You may invest the money in your IRA or self-employed plan retirement account (SEP-IRAs and so on) in stocks, bonds, mutual funds, and some other common investments, including bank accounts. Mutual funds (offered in most employer-based plans) and exchange-traded funds (ETFs) are ideal choices because they offer diversification and professional management. See the "Buying stocks via mutual funds and exchange-traded funds" section later in this chapter for more on mutual funds and ETFs.

Annuities: Maxing out your retirement savings

What if you have so much cash sitting around that after maxing out your contributions to retirement accounts, including your IRA, you still want to sock more away into a tax-advantaged account? Enter the annuity. *Annuities* are contracts that insurance companies back. If you, the investor (annuity holder), should die during the so-called accumulation phase (that is, before receiving payments from the annuity), your designated beneficiary is guaranteed reimbursement of the amount of your original investment.

Annuities, like IRAs, allow your capital to grow and compound tax-deferred. You defer taxes until you withdraw the money. Unlike an IRA, which has an annual contribution limit of a few thousand dollars, an annuity allows you to deposit as much as you want in any year — even millions of dollars, if you've got millions! As with a Roth IRA, however, you get no up-front tax deduction for your contributions.

WARNING

Because annuity contributions aren't tax-deductible, and because annuities carry higher annual operating fees to pay for the small amount of insurance that comes with them, don't consider contributing to one until you've fully exhausted your other retirement account investing options. Because of their higher annual expenses, annuities generally make sense only if you won't need the money for 15 or more years.

Transferring retirement accounts

Except for plans maintained by your current employer that limit your investment options, such as most 401(k)s, you can move your money held in an SEP-IRA, a self-employed 401(k), a traditional IRA, and many 403(b) plans (also known as *tax-sheltered annuities*) or 401(k) plans you hold at former employers to almost any major investment firm. Moving the money is pretty simple: If you can fill out some forms online or send them back in a postage-paid envelope, you can transfer an account. The investment firm to which you're transferring your account does the rest.

Transferring accounts you control

Here's a step-by-step list of what you need to do to transfer a retirement account to another investment firm. Even if you're working with a financial advisor, you should be aware of this process (called a *direct trustee-to-trustee transfer*) to ensure that no hanky-panky takes place on the advisor's part and to ensure that the transfer is not taxable.

1. **Decide where you want to move the account.**

   You may also want to consult the latest editions of some of my other books, including *Mutual Funds For Dummies* and *Investing For Dummies* (Wiley) and visit my website at www.erictyson.com.

2. Obtain an account application and asset transfer form.

Call the toll-free number of the firm you're transferring the money to and ask for an *account application and asset transfer form* for the type of account you're transferring — for example, SEP-IRA, self-employed 401(k), IRA, 403(b), or 401(k). You can also visit the firm's website, but for this type of request, I think most people find it easier to speak directly to someone.

TIP

Ask for the form for the same type of account you currently have at the company from which you're transferring the money. You can determine the account type by looking at a recent account statement — the account type should appear near the top of the statement or in the section with your name and address. If you can't figure out the account type on a cryptic statement, call the firm where the account is currently held and ask a representative to tell you what kind of account you have.

WARNING

Never, ever sign over assets such as checks and security certificates to a financial advisor, no matter how trustworthy and honest they may seem. Transfers should not be completed this way. The advisor can bolt with them quicker than you can say "Bonnie and Clyde." Besides, you'll find the transfer easier by following the information in this section.

3. Figure out which securities you want to transfer and which need to be liquidated.

Transferring existing investments in your account to a new investment firm can sometimes be a little sticky. Transferring such assets as cash (money-market funds) or securities that trade on any of the major stock exchanges is not a problem.

TIP

If you own publicly traded securities, transferring them as is (also known as transferring them *in kind*) to your new investment firm is better, especially if the firm offers discount brokerage services. You can then sell your securities through that firm more cheaply.

If you own mutual funds unique to the institution you're leaving, check with your new firm to see whether it can accept them. If not, you need to contact the firm that currently holds them to sell them.

Certificates of deposit are tricky to transfer. Ideally, you should send in the transfer forms several weeks or so before the CDs mature. If the CD matures soon, call the bank and tell it that when the CD matures, you would like the funds to be invested in a savings or money-market account that you can access without penalty when your transfer request lands in the bank's mailbox.

4. **Complete and mail the account application and asset transfer form.**

   Completing these for your new investment firm opens your new account and authorizes the transfer.

WARNING

   Don't take possession of the money in your retirement account when moving it over to the new firm. The tax authorities impose huge penalties if you perform a transfer incorrectly. Let the company to which you're transferring the money do the transfer for you. If you have questions or problems, the firm(s) to which you're transferring your account has capable employees waiting to help you. Remember, these firms know that you're transferring your money to them, so they should roll out the red carpet.

5. **Let the firm from which you're transferring the money know that you're doing so. (This step is optional.)**

   If the place you're transferring the money from doesn't assign a specific person to your account, you can definitely skip this step. When you're moving your investments from a broker-age firm where you dealt with a particular broker, deciding whether to follow this step can be more difficult.

   Most people feel obligated to let their representative know that they're moving their money. In my experience, calling the person with the "bad news" is usually a mistake. Brokers or others who have a direct financial stake in your decision to move your money will try to convince you to stay. Some may try to make you feel guilty for leaving, and some may even try to bully you.

TIP

   Writing an email or letter may seem like the coward's way out, but writing usually makes leaving your broker easier for both of you. You can polish what you have to say, and you don't put the broker on the defensive. Although I don't want to encourage lying, not telling the *whole* truth may be an even better idea. Excuses, such as that you have a family member in the investment business who will manage your money, may help you avoid an uncomfortable confrontation.

Then again, telling an investment firm that its fees are too high or that it misrepresented and sold you a bunch of lousy investments may help the firm improve in the future. Don't fret too much — do what's best for you and what you're comfortable with. Brokers are not your friends. Even though the broker may know your kids' names, your favorite hobbies, and your birthday, you have a *business* relationship with that broker.

Transferring your existing assets typically takes two to four weeks to complete. If the transfer is not completed within one month, get in touch with your new investment firm to determine the problem. If your old company isn't cooperating, call a manager there to help get the ball rolling.

The unfortunate reality is that an investment firm will cheerfully set up a new account to *accept* your money on a moment's notice, but it will drag its feet, sometimes for months, when the time comes to relinquish your money. To light a fire under the behinds of the folks at the investment firm, tell a manager at the old firm that you're going to send letters to the Financial Industry Regulatory Authority (FINRA) www.finra.com/contact_us and the Securities and Exchange Commission (SEC) www.sec.gov/ if it doesn't complete your transfer within the next week.

Moving money from an employer's plan

When you leave a job, you're confronted with a slightly different transfer challenge: moving money from an employer plan into one of your own retirement accounts. (As long as your employer allows it, you may be able to leave your money in your old employer's plan.) Typically, employer retirement plan money can be rolled over into your own IRA. Check with your employer's benefits department or a tax advisor for details.

WARNING

Federal tax law requires employers to withhold, as a tax, 20 percent of any retirement account disbursements to plan participants. So if you personally take possession of your retirement account money in order to transfer it to an IRA, you must wait until you file your annual tax return to be reimbursed by the government for this 20 percent withholding. This withholding creates a problem, because if you don't replace the 20 percent withholding into the rollover IRA and deposit the entire rollover within 60 days in the new account, the IRS treats the shortfall as an early distribution subject to income tax and penalties.

TIP

Never take personal possession of money from your employer's retirement plan. To avoid the 20 percent tax withholding and a lot of other hassles, inform your employer of where you want your money to be sent. Prior to doing so, establish an appropriate account (an IRA, for example) at the investment firm you intend to use. Then tell your employer's benefits department where you'd like your retirement money transferred. You can send your employer a copy of your account statement, which contains the investment firm's mailing address and your account number.

Patience and Persistence: The Tortoise Beats the Day Trader

Stocks are intended to be long-term holdings. When you buy stocks, you should plan to hold them for at least five years or more — and preferably seven to ten. When stocks suffer a setback, it may take months or even years for them to come back.

When you invest in stocks, many (perhaps too many) choices exist. Besides the tens of thousands of stocks from which you can select, you also can invest in mutual funds, exchange-traded funds (ETFs), or hedge funds, or you can have a stockbroker select for you.

REMEMBER

Anybody, no matter what their educational background, IQ, occupation, income, or assets, can make solid returns through stock investments. Over long periods of time, based on historic performance, you can expect to earn an average of about 9 percent per year total return by investing in stocks.

Making money from stocks

When you purchase shares of a company's stock, you can profit from your ownership in two ways:

>> **Dividends:** Most stocks pay dividends. Companies generally make some profits during the year. Some high-growth companies reinvest most or all of their profits right back into the business. However, many companies pay out some of their profits to shareholders in the form of quarterly *dividends.*

>> **Appreciation:** When the price per share of your stock rises to a level greater than you originally paid for it, you make money. This profit, however, is only on paper until you sell the stock, at which time you realize a *capital gain*. (Such gains realized over periods longer than one year are taxed at the lower long-term capital gains tax rate.) Of course, the stock price per share can fall below what you originally paid as well (in which case you have a loss on paper unless you realize that loss by selling).

If you add together dividends and appreciation, you arrive at your total return. Stocks differ in the dimensions of these possible returns, particularly with respect to dividends.

Buying stocks via mutual funds and exchange-traded funds

If you're busy and suffer no delusions about your expertise, you'll love the best stock mutual funds. Investing in stocks through mutual funds can be as simple as dialing a toll-free phone number or logging on to a fund company's website, completing application forms, and zapping them some money.

Mutual funds take money invested by people like you and me and pool it in a single investment portfolio in securities, such as stocks and bonds. The portfolio is then professionally managed. Stock mutual funds, as the name suggests, invest primarily or exclusively in stocks (some stock funds sometimes invest a bit in other stuff, such as bonds).

Exchange-traded funds (ETFs) are in many ways similar to mutual funds, specifically index funds, except that they trade on a stock exchange. One potential attraction is that some ETFs offer investors the potential for even lower operating expenses than comparable mutual funds and may be tax-friendlier.

Stock funds include many advantages:

REMEMBER

>> **Diversification:** Buying individual stocks on your own is relatively time-consuming and costly unless you buy reasonable chunks (100 shares or so) of each stock. But to buy 100 shares each in, say, a dozen companies' stocks to ensure diversification, you need about $60,000 if the stocks that you buy average $50 per share.

>> **Professional management:** Even if you have big bucks to invest, funds offer something that you can't deliver: professional, full-time management. Fund managers peruse a company's financial statements and otherwise track and analyze its business strategy and market position. The best managers put in long hours and possess lots of expertise and experience in the field. (If you've been misled into believing that with minimal effort, you can rack up market-beating returns by selecting your own stocks, please be sure to read the rest of this chapter.)

Look at it this way: Funds are a huge time-saver. On your next day off, would you rather sit in front of your computer and research semiconductors and paper manufacturers, or would you rather enjoy dinner or a movie with family and friends? (The answer to that question depends on who your family and friends are!)

>> **Low costs — if you pick 'em right:** To convince you that funds aren't a good way for you to invest, those with a vested interest, such as stock-picking newsletter pundits, may point out the high fees that some funds charge. An element of truth rings here: Some funds are expensive, charging you a couple percent or more per year in operating expenses on top of hefty sales commissions.

But just as you wouldn't want to invest in a fund that a novice with no track record manages, why would you want to invest in a high-cost fund? Contrary to the "You get what you pay for" notion often trumpeted by those trying to sell you something at an inflated price, some of the best managers are the cheapest to hire. Through a *no-load* (commission-free) mutual fund, you can hire a professional, full-time money manager to invest $10,000 for a mere $20 to $100 per year. Some index funds and exchange-traded funds charge even less.

As with all investments, funds have some drawbacks. Consider the following:

>> **The issue of control is a problem for some investors.** If you like feeling in control, sending your investment dollars to a seemingly black-box process where others decide when and in what to invest your money may unnerve you. However, you need to be more concerned about the

potential blunders that you may make investing in individual stocks of your own choosing or, even worse, those stocks pitched to you by a broker. And the financial markets can change fast, challenge your recent thinking, stress you out, and quickly make you feel like you're actually not in control!

>> **Taxes are a concern when you invest in funds outside of retirement accounts.** Because the fund manager decides when to sell specific stock holdings, some funds may produce more taxable distributions. That doesn't rule out investing in funds, however, as there are some really good tax-friendly funds.

Using hedge funds and privately managed funds

Like mutual funds, *hedge funds* are managed investment vehicles. In other words, an investment management team researches and manages the funds' portfolio. However, hedge funds are oriented to affluent investors and typically charge steep fees — a 1.0 to 1.5 percent annual management fee plus a 15 to 20 percent cut of the annual fund returns.

No proof exists that hedge funds as a group perform better than mutual funds. In fact, the objective studies that I've reviewed show inferior hedge fund returns, which makes sense. Those high hedge fund fees depress their returns. Notwithstanding the small number of hedge funds that have produced better long-term returns, too many affluent folks invest in hedge funds due to the fund's hyped marketing and the badge of exclusivity they offer.

WARNING

Please be aware that there is a surplus of various hedge/private investment managers who are small players in the investment management world. These folks write blogs, preen on social media, and serve as "experts" and "gurus" in other media, where they make all sorts of unsubstantiated and unverified claims. The common thread of such claims, as you may guess, is how awesome these folks are in supposedly having seen what was coming in the financial markets and supposedly positioning their clients' investment holdings well, leading to the production of high returns. This fibbing is enabled by the fact that private money managers and hedge fund managers don't have public performance data requirements.

Selecting individual stocks yourself

More than a few investing gurus and books suggest and enthusiastically encourage people to do their own stock picking. However, the vast majority of investors are better off *not* picking their own stocks, in my observations and experience.

I've long been an advocate of educating yourself and taking responsibility for your own financial affairs, but taking responsibility for your finances doesn't mean you should do *everything* yourself. Table 6-1 includes some thoughts to consider about choosing your own stocks.

TABLE 6-1 **Why You're Buying Your Own Stocks**

Good Reasons to Pick Your Own Stocks	Bad Reasons to Pick Your Own Stocks
You enjoy the challenge.	You think you can beat the best money managers. (If you can, you're probably in the wrong profession!)
You want to learn more about business.	You want more control over your investments, which you think may happen if you understand the companies that you invest in.
You possess a substantial amount of money to invest.	You think that mutual funds are for people who aren't smart enough to choose their own stocks.
You're a buy-and-hold investor.	You're attracted to the ability to trade your stocks anytime you want.

Some popular investing blogs, websites, and books try to convince investors that they can do a *better* job than the professionals at picking their own stocks. Amateur investors, however, need to devote a lot of study to become proficient at stock selection. Many professional investors work 60+ hours a week at investing, but you're unlikely to be willing to spend that much time on it. Don't let the popularity of those do-it-yourself stock-picking online gurus and books lead you astray.

REMEMBER

Choosing a stock isn't as simple as visiting a restaurant chain (or buying a pair of shoes or an iGadget), liking it, buying its stock, and then sitting back and getting rich watching your stock zoom to the moon. I've had investing ideas myself for picking individual stocks, and if I had acted on them, I would have done very well in some cases and terribly in others. Thanks to the decades of my adult life and observing the financial markets, I know that stock picking is much harder than most people think it is.

If you invest in stocks, I think you know by now that guarantees don't exist. But as in many of life's endeavors, you can buy individual stocks in good and not-so-good ways. So if you want to select your own individual stocks, check out the most recent edition of my book *Investing For Dummies* (Wiley), where I explain how to best research and trade them.

Proven investment strategies

TIP

To maximize your chances of stock market investment success, do the following:

>> **Don't try to time the markets.** Anticipating where the stock market and specific stocks are heading is next to impossible, especially over the short term. Economic factors, which are influenced by thousands of elements as well as human emotions, determine stock market prices. Be a regular buyer of stocks with new savings. As I discuss earlier in this chapter, consider buying more stocks when they're on sale and market pessimism is running high. Don't make the mistake of bailing out when the market is down!

>> **Diversify your investments.** Invest in the stocks of different-sized companies in varying industries around the world. When assessing your investments' performance, examine your whole portfolio at least once a year, and calculate your total return after expenses and trading fees. To read more about ways to diversify your investments, see the later section "Diversification: Not Putting All Your Eggs in One Basket."

>> **Keep trading costs, management fees, and commissions to a minimum.** These costs represent a big drain on your returns. If you invest through an individual broker or a financial advisor who earns a living on commissions, odds are that you're paying more than you need to be. And you're likely receiving biased advice, too.

>> **Pay attention to taxes.** Like commissions and fees, federal and state taxes are a major investment "expense" that you can minimize. Contribute most of your money to your tax-advantaged retirement accounts. You can invest your

money outside of retirement accounts, but keep an eye on taxes. Calculate your annual returns on an *after*-tax basis.

>> **Don't overestimate your ability to pick the big-winning stocks.** One of the best ways to invest in stocks is through mutual funds and exchange-traded funds, which allow you to use an experienced, full-time money manager at a low cost to perform all the investing grunt work for you.

Avoiding problematic stock-buying practices

You may be curious about ways to buy individual stocks, but note that if the methods you're curious about appear in the following list, it's because I *don't* recommend using them. You can greatly increase your chances of success and earn higher returns if you avoid the commonly made stock-investing mistakes that I present next.

>> **Beware of broker conflicts of interest:** Some investors make the mistake of investing in individual stocks through a broker who earns commissions. The standard pitch from these firms and their brokers is that they maintain research departments that monitor and report on stocks. Their brokers, using this research, tell you when and what to buy, sell, or hold. Sounds good in theory, but this system has significant problems.

WARNING

Many brokerage firms happen to be in another business that creates enormous conflicts of interest in producing objective company reviews. These investment firms also solicit companies to help them sell new stock and bond issues. To gain this business, the brokerage firms need to demonstrate enthusiasm and optimism for the company's future prospects.

Brokerage analysts who, with the best of intentions, write negative reports about a company find their careers hindered in a variety of ways. Some firms fire such analysts. Companies that the analysts criticize exclude those analysts from analyst meetings about the company. So most analysts who know what's good for their careers and their brokerage firms don't write disapproving reports (but some do take chances).

>> **Don't short-term trade or try to time the market:**
Unfortunately (for themselves), some investors track their
stock investments closely and believe they need to sell after
short holding periods — months, weeks, or even days. With
the growth of internet and computerized trading, such
shortsightedness has taken a turn for the worse as more
investors now engage in a foolish process known as *day
trading,* where they buy and sell a stock within the same day!

Stocks are intended to be long-term holdings. You shouldn't
buy stocks if you don't plan to hold them for at least five
years or more — and preferably seven to ten. When stocks
suffer a setback, it may take months or even years for them
to come back.

>> **Be wary of gurus:** It's tempting to want to consult a guru
who claims to be able to foresee an impending major decline
and get you out of an investment before it tanks. Believe me
when I say that plenty of these pundits are talking up such
supposed prowess. The financial crisis of 2008 brought an
avalanche of prognosticators out of the woodwork claiming
that if you had been listening to them, you could have not
only side-stepped losses but also made money.

From having researched many such claims (see the "Guru
Watch" section of my website, www.erictyson.com), I can
tell you that nearly all these folks significantly misrepresented their past predictions and recommendations. And the
few who made some halfway decent predictions in the
recent short term had poor or unremarkable longer-term
track records.

>> **Shun penny stocks:** Thousands of smaller-company stocks
trade on the over-the-counter *penny stocks* market. Some of
these companies are quite small and sport low prices per
share that range from pennies to several dollars, hence the
name *penny stocks.*

The biggest problem with buying penny stocks is that some
are grossly overpriced, often due to dishonest practices by
individual brokers or brokerage firms. Just as you don't
make good investment returns by purchasing jewelry that's
marked up 100 percent, you don't have a fighting chance to
make decent money on penny stocks that the broker may
flog with similar markups.

Diversification: Not Putting All Your Eggs in One Basket

Diversification is one of the most powerful investment concepts. It refers to saving your eggs (or investments) in different baskets. Diversification requires you to place your money in different investments with returns that are not completely correlated, which is a fancy way of saying that when some of your investments are down in value, odds are that others are up in value.

TIP

To decrease the chances of all your investments getting clobbered at the same time, you must put your money in different types of investments, such as bonds, stocks, real estate, and small business. You can further diversify your investments by investing in domestic as well as international markets.

Within a given class of investments, such as stocks, investing in different types of that class (such as different types of stocks) that perform well under various economic conditions is important. For this reason, *mutual funds*, which are diversified portfolios of securities such as stocks or bonds, are a highly useful investment vehicle, as are exchange-traded funds (ETFs), which are like mutual funds but trade on a stock exchange. When you buy into a mutual fund, your money is pooled with the money of many others and invested in a vast array of stocks or bonds.

You can look at the benefits of diversification in two ways:

>> Diversification reduces the volatility in the value of your whole portfolio. In other words, your portfolio can achieve the same rate of return that a single investment can provide with less fluctuation in value.

>> Diversification allows you to obtain a higher rate of return for a given level of risk.

REMEMBER

Keep in mind that no one, no matter whom they work for or what credentials they have, can guarantee returns on an investment. You can do good research and get lucky, but no one is free from the risk of losing money.

Spreading the wealth: Asset allocation

Asset allocation refers to how you spread your investing dollars among different investment choices (stocks, bonds, money-market accounts, and so on). Before you can intelligently decide how to allocate your assets, you need to ponder a number of issues, including your present financial situation, your goals and priorities, and the pros and cons of various investment alternatives.

Although stocks and real estate offer attractive long-term returns, they can sometimes suffer significant declines. Thus, these investments are not suitable for money that you think you may want or need to use within, say, the next five years.

Money-market and shorter-term bond investments are good places to keep money that you expect to use soon. Everyone should have a reserve of money — about three to six months' worth of living expenses in a money-market fund — that's accessible in an emergency. Shorter-term bonds or bond mutual funds can serve as a higher-yielding, secondary emergency cushion. (See Chapter 2 for more on emergency reserves.)

Bonds can also be useful for some longer-term investing for diversification purposes. For example, when investing for retirement, placing a portion of your money in bonds helps buffer stock market declines.

Allocating money for the long term

Investing money for retirement is a classic long-term goal for most people. Your current age and the number of years until you expect to need the money and retire are the biggest factors to consider when allocating money for long-term purposes. The younger you are and the more years you have before retirement, the more comfortable you can afford to be with growth-oriented (and more volatile) investments, such as stocks and investment real estate.

One useful guideline for dividing or allocating your money between longer-term-oriented growth investments, such as stocks, and more-conservative lending investments, such as bonds, is to subtract your age from 110 (or 120 if you want to be aggressive; 100 to be more conservative) and invest the resulting percentage in stocks. You then invest the remaining amount in bonds.

For example, if you're 30 years old, you invest from 70 (100 – 30) to 90 (120 – 30) percent in stocks. You invest the remaining 10 to 30 percent in bonds.

Table 6-2 lists some guidelines for allocating long-term money based on your age and the level of risk you desire.

TABLE 6-2 Allocating Long-Term Money

Your Investment Attitude	Bond Allocation (%)	Stock Allocation (%)
Play it safer	= Age	= 100 – age
Middle-of-the-road	= Age – 10	= 110 – age
Aggressive	= Age – 20	= 120 – age

For example, if you're the conservative sort who doesn't like a lot of risk but recognizes the value of striving for some growth and making your money work harder, you're a *middle-of-the-road* type. Using Table 6-2, if you're 40 years old, you may consider putting 30 percent (40 – 10) in bonds and 70 percent (110 – 40) in stocks.

In most employer retirement plans, mutual funds are the typical investment vehicle. If your employer's retirement plan includes more than one stock mutual fund as an option, you can try discerning which options are best by using the criteria I discuss in my book *Investing For Dummies* (Wiley). In the event that all your retirement plan's stock fund options are good, you can simply divide your stock allocation among the choices.

TIP

When one or more of the choices is an international stock fund, consider allocating a percentage of your stock fund money to overseas investments: at least 20 percent for play-it-safe investors, 25 to 35 percent for middle-of-the-road investors, and as much as 35 to 50 percent for aggressive investors.

If the 40-year-old middle-of-the-roader from the previous example is investing 70 percent in stocks, about 25 to 35 percent of the stock fund investments (which works out to be about 18 to 24 percent of the total) can be invested in international stock funds.

Sticking with your allocations: Don't trade

Your goals and desire to take risk should drive the allocation of your investment dollars. As you get older, gradually scaling back on the riskiness (and therefore growth potential and volatility) of your portfolio generally makes sense.

Don't tinker with your portfolio daily, weekly, monthly, or even annually. (Every two to three years or so, you may want to rebalance your holdings to get your mix to a desired asset allocation, as discussed in the preceding section.) Don't engage in trading with the hopes of buying into a hot investment and selling your losers. Jumping onto a "winner" and dumping a "loser" may provide some short-term psychological comfort, but in the long term, such an investment strategy often produces below-average returns.

WARNING

When an investment gets front-page coverage and everyone is talking about its stunning rise, it's definitely time to take a reality check. The higher an investment's price rises, the greater the danger that it's overpriced. Its next move may be downward. Don't follow the herd.

Investing lump sums via dollar-cost averaging

When you have what is to you a large chunk of cash to invest — whether you received it from an accumulation of funds over the years, an inheritance, or a recent windfall from work you've done — you may have a problem deciding what to do with it. Many people, of course, would like to have your problem. (You're not complaining, right?) You want to invest your money, but you're a bit skittish — if not outright terrified — at the prospect of investing the lump of money all at once.

REMEMBER

If the money is residing in a savings or money-market account, you may feel like it's wasting away. You want to put it to work! My first words of advice are "Don't rush." Nothing is wrong with earning a small return in a money-market account. Remember that a money-market fund beats the heck out of rushing into an investment in which you may lose 20 percent or more. When I worked as a financial advisor, I sometimes got calls from people in a state of near panic. Typically, these folks had CDs coming due, and they felt that they needed to decide exactly where they wanted to invest the money in the 48 hours before the CD matured.

TIP

Take a deep breath. You have absolutely no reason to rush into an important decision. Tell your friendly banker that when the CD matures, you want to put the proceeds into the bank's highest-yielding savings or money-market account. That way, your money continues to earn interest while you buy yourself some breathing room.

One approach to investing is called *dollar-cost averaging* (DCA). With DCA, you invest your money in equal chunks on a regular basis — such as once a month — into a diversified group of investments. For example, if you have $60,000 to invest, you can invest $2,500 per month until it's all invested, which takes a couple of years. The money awaiting future investment isn't lying fallow; you keep it in a money-market account so it can earn a bit of interest while waiting its turn.

The attraction of DCA is that it allows you to ease into riskier investments instead of jumping in all at once. If the price of the investment drops after some of your initial purchases, you can buy some later at a lower price. If you dump your entire chunk of money into an investment all at once and then it drops like a stone, you'll be kicking yourself for not waiting.

The flip side of DCA is that when your investment of choice appreciates in value, you may wish that you had invested your money faster. Another drawback of DCA is that you may get cold feet as you continue to pour money into an investment that's dropping in value.

DCA can also cause headaches with your taxes when the time comes to sell investments held outside retirement accounts. When you buy an investment at many different times and prices, the accounting becomes muddied as you sell blocks of the investment.

TIP

DCA is most valuable when the money you want to invest represents a large portion of your total assets and you can stick to a schedule. Make DCA automatic so you're less likely to abandon plans if the investment falls after your initial purchases.

Chapter **7**

Setting Financial Goals Beyond Paying Bills

n my work as a financial counselor, I always asked new clients what their short- and long-term personal and financial goals were. Most people reported that reflecting on these questions was incredibly valuable, because they hadn't considered it for a long time — if ever.

In this chapter, I help you consider what you want to get out of life. Although my expertise is in personal finance, I wouldn't be doing my job if I didn't get you to consider your nonfinancial goals and how money fits into the rest of your life goals. So, before I jump into how to establish and save toward common financial goals, I discuss how to think about making and saving money, as well as how to best fit your financial goals into the rest of your life.

Dreaming of Financial Independence

If you hope to someday reduce the time you spend working or cease working altogether, you'll need sufficient savings to support yourself. Many people — particularly young people and those who don't work well with numbers — underestimate the amount of money needed to retire. To figure out how much you should save per month to achieve your retirement goals, you need to crunch a few numbers. (Don't worry — this number-crunching is usually easier than doing your taxes.)

Luckily for you, you don't have to start cold. Studies show how people typically spend money before and during retirement. Most people need about 70 to 80 percent of their pre-retirement income throughout retirement to maintain their standard of living. For example, if your household earns $70,000 per year before retirement, you're likely to need $49,000 to $56,000 (70 to 80 percent of $70,000) per year during retirement to live the way you're accustomed to living. The 70 to 80 percent range is an average. Some people may need more simply because they have more time on their hands to spend their money. Others adjust their standard of living and live on less.

TIP

So how do you figure out what you're going to need? The following three profiles provide a rough estimate of the percentage of your pre-retirement income that you're going to need during retirement. Pick the one that most accurately describes your situation. If you fall between two descriptions, pick a percentage in between those two.

To maintain your standard of living in retirement, you may need about

>> **65 percent of your pre-retirement income if you**

- Save a large amount (15 percent or more) of your annual earnings

- Are a high-income earner

- Will own your home debt-free by the time you retire

- Do not anticipate leading a lifestyle in retirement that reflects your current high income

If you're an especially high-income earner who lives well beneath your means, you may be able to do just fine with even less than 65 percent. Pick an annual dollar amount or percentage of your current income that will allow the kind of retirement lifestyle you desire.

>> **75 percent of your pre-retirement income if you**

- Save a reasonable amount (5 to 14 percent) of your annual earnings

- Will still have some mortgage debt or a modest rent to pay by the time you retire

- Anticipate having a standard of living in retirement that's comparable to what you have today

>> **85 percent of your pre-retirement income if you**

- Save little or none of your annual earnings (less than 5 percent)

- Will have a relatively significant mortgage payment or sizeable rent to pay in retirement

- Anticipate wanting or needing to maintain your current lifestyle throughout retirement

Knowing What's Most Important to You

Unless you earn really big bucks or have a large family inheritance to fall back on, your personal and financial desires will probably outstrip your resources. Thus, you need to prioritize your goals.

One of the biggest mistakes I see people make is rushing into a financial decision without considering what's really important to them. Because many people get caught up in the responsibilities of their daily lives, they often don't have time for reflection.

TIP

As a result of my experience counseling and teaching people about better personal financial management, I can tell you that the folks who accomplish their goals aren't necessarily smarter or higher-income earners than those who don't. People who identify their goals and then work toward them, which often requires changing some habits, are the ones who accomplish their goals.

See whether any of the following reflect your ambitions:

>> **Owning your home:** Renting and dealing with landlords can be a financial and emotional drag, so most folks want to buy into the American dream and own some real estate — the most basic of which is your own home.

>> **Making major purchases:** Most folks need to plan ahead for major purchases such as a car, living room furniture, vacations, and so on.

>> **Retiring/Achieving financial independence:** No, retiring doesn't imply sitting on a rocking chair watching the world go by while hoping that some long-lost friend, your son's or daughter's family, or the neighborhood dog comes by to visit. *Retiring* is a catchall term for discontinuing full-time work or perhaps not even working for pay at all. Some folks find the concept of "financial independence" more to their liking because it conveys reaching a level of financial security where you no longer have to work full time or perhaps at all.

>> **Educating the kids:** All those diaper changes, late-night feedings, and trips to the zoo aren't enough to get Junior out of your house and into the real world as a productive, self-sufficient adult. You may want to help your children get a college education or some other form of higher education or skill training.

>> **Owning your own business:** Many employees want to take on the challenges and rewards that come with being the boss. The primary reason that most people continue just to dream is that they lack the money to leave their primary job. Although many businesses don't require gobs of start-up cash, almost all require that you withstand a substantial reduction in your income during the early years.

Because everyone is different, you can have goals (other than those in the preceding list) that are unique to your own situation. Accomplishing such goals almost always requires saving money. One of my favorite proverbs says "Do not wait until you are thirsty to dig a well," so don't wait to save money until you're ready to accomplish a personal or financial goal!

Valuing retirement accounts

Where possible, try to save and invest in accounts that offer you a tax advantage, which is precisely what retirement accounts do. These accounts — known by such enlightening acronyms and names as 401(k), 403(b), SEP-IRAs, and so on — offer tax breaks to people of all economic means. Consider the following advantages to investing in retirement accounts:

>> **Contributions are usually tax-deductible.** By putting money in a retirement account, not only do you plan wisely for your future, but you also get an immediate financial reward: lower taxes, which means more money available for

saving and investing. Retirement account contributions generally aren't taxed at either the federal or state income-tax level until withdrawal (but they're still subject to Social Security and Medicare taxes when earned). If you're paying, say, 30 percent between federal and state taxes (see Chapter 5 to determine your tax bracket), a $5,000 contribution to a retirement account lowers your taxes by $1,500.

>> **In some company retirement accounts, companies match a portion of your own contributions.** Thus, in addition to tax breaks, you get free extra money courtesy of your employer!

>> **Returns on your investment compound over time without taxation.** After you put money into a retirement account, any interest, dividends, and appreciation add to your account without being taxed. Of course, there's no such thing as a free lunch — these accounts don't allow for complete tax avoidance. Yet, you can get a really great lunch at a discount: You get to defer taxes on all the accumulating gains and profits until you withdraw the money down the road. Thus, more money is working for you over a longer period of time. (The Roth IRA offers no up-front tax breaks but does allow future tax-free withdrawal of investment earnings.)

The tax rates on stock dividends and *long-term capital gains* (investments held more than one year) are lower than the tax rates levied on ordinary income (such as that earned through working). This fact makes some people think that investing through retirement accounts may not be worthwhile because all investment earnings are taxed at the relatively high ordinary income-tax rates when money is withdrawn from retirement accounts. I'll cut to the chase: The vast majority of people are better off contributing to retirement accounts.

Dealing with competing goals

Unless you enjoy paying higher taxes, why would you save money outside of retirement accounts, which shelter your money from taxation? The reason is that some financial goals are not easily achieved by saving in retirement accounts. Also, retirement accounts have caps on the amount you can contribute annually.

If you're accumulating money for a down payment on a home or to start or buy a business, for example, you'll probably need to save that money outside of a retirement account. Why? Because with limited exceptions, if you withdraw funds from retirement accounts before age 59½, not only do you have to pay income taxes on the withdrawals, but you also generally have to pay *early withdrawal penalties* of 10 percent of the withdrawn amount in federal tax plus whatever your state charges.

REMEMBER

Because you're constrained by your financial resources, you need to prioritize your goals. Before funding your retirement accounts and racking up those tax breaks, consider your other goals.

Saving for big purchases

If you want to buy a car, the latest smartphone, or a vacation to Thailand, do not — I repeat, do not — buy such things with *consumer credit* (that is, by incurring and carrying debt from month to month to finance the purchase on a credit card or auto loan). As I explain in Chapter 3, cars, boats, vacations, and the like are consumer items, not wealth-building investments, such as real estate or small businesses. A car begins to depreciate the moment you drive it off the sales lot. Money spent on a vacation is worthless the moment you arrive back home. (I know your memories will be priceless, but they won't pay the bills.)

TIP

Don't deny yourself gratification; just learn how to delay or modify it. Get into the habit of saving for your larger consumer purchases to avoid paying for them over time with high-interest consumer credit. When saving up for a consumer purchase such as a car, a money-market account or short-term bond fund is a good place to store your short-term savings.

Paying for high-interest consumer debt can cripple your ability not only to save for long-term goals but also to make major purchases in the future. Interest on consumer debt is exorbitantly expensive — upwards of 20 percent on credit cards. When contemplating the purchase of a consumer item on credit, add up the total interest you'd end up paying on your debt and call it the price of instant gratification.

Avoiding Over-Saving

Yes, it's true: Over-saving is possible. Some people, in fact often the best savers, get hooked on amassing more and more money and have trouble enjoying and using their money. Super savers and money amassers generally equate more money with more financial security.

If you don't have this problem of over-saving, and you think that this is like hearing about someone complaining that they have too much caviar, please consider reading on — you may have loved ones, friends, or other contacts who suffer from this problematic issue!

This section can help you address and temper this mindset.

Understanding the over-saver mindset

Just as some people think that their financial problems would be solved if only they could earn a higher income, over-savers typically believe that if they could reach a greater level of assets, they'd be more relaxed and could do what they really want with their lives. The bar, however, continually gets raised, and the level of "enough" is rarely attained. For this reason, some of the best savers and money accumulators also have the most difficulty spending money, even in retirement.

Some super savers have insecurities relating to money. Specifically, they view amassing financial assets as providing them with safety and security that extend far beyond the financial realm. While having more financial assets, in theory, provides greater financial peace of mind, these riches don't necessarily provide more of the other types of security — friendships, for example, for which hoarders are searching.

REMEMBER

When money hoarders marry people with significantly different money personalities, fireworks ensue, and divorce may be the result. Financial security doesn't translate into emotional security and contentment.

Achieving a certain level of affluence can provide greater access to quality healthcare. However, once one reaches the point at which quality healthcare is the norm, the incessant pursuit of more money can have a negative impact on an individual's long-term health and quality of life. For example, super savers often believe that they will be better protected as seniors and better able to enjoy their retirement years with hefty account balances. But the pursuit of more money, which typically entails longer work hours and greater stress, can lead to more health problems before and in retirement.

Many super savers, who also tend to be obsessed with work, come from homes and families where they felt on the edge economically and emotionally. Although there are so many things that we can't control in the world, money amassers typically derive a sense of both economic and emotional security from saving a lot of money.

Super savers have an amazing ability to selectively hear particular stories that reinforce rather than question their tendencies and beliefs. For example, stories periodically surface about how the legions of baby boomers retiring will bankrupt Social Security and cause a stock market collapse. Super savers batten down the hatches, save more, and invest even more conservatively when such stories worry them. News stories about stock market declines, corporate layoffs, budget deficits, terrorism risks, rising energy prices, and conflicts in the Middle East and elsewhere cause super savers to close their wallets, clutch their investments, and worry and save more.

Balancing spending and saving

Most people don't want to work their entire adulthood. And, even if they do enjoy working for pay that much, who wants to live on the edge economically, always dependent upon the next paycheck to be able to pay the monthly bills?

That's why you should avoid the extremes of overspending and over-saving. Consider the analogy to eating food: Eat too little or not enough of the right kinds of foods and you go hungry and possibly suffer deficiencies of energy and nutrition; too much eating, on the other hand, leads to obesity and other health problems.

Overspending and its companion, under-saving, hamper your ability to accomplish future personal and financial goals, and in the worst cases, can lead to bankruptcy. Over-saving can lead to not living in the moment and constantly postponing for tomorrows that we may not live to enjoy.

Remember Goldilocks and her quest at the bear's home for the bowl of porridge that was not too hot and not too cold and a bed to rest in that was not too hard and not too soft? Everyone should save money as a cushion and to accomplish important personal and financial goals.

Keeping money accumulation in proper perspective

As with any good habit, you can get too much of a good thing. Washing your hands and maintaining proper hygiene is worthwhile, but it becomes problematic when you obsess over cleanliness and it interferes with your life and personal relationships.

Conquering over-saving and an obsession with money typically requires a mix of education and specific incremental behavioral changes. Substantive change typically comes over months and years, not days and weeks.

The vast majority of super savers work many hours and may neglect their loved ones and themselves. They typically need to work less and lead more balanced lives. That may involve changing jobs or careers or simply coming up with a "stop-doing list," the opposite of a "to-do list."

Giving yourself permission to spend more

Money amassers usually need to discover how to loosen the purse strings. Figuring out how to spend more and save less is a problem more folks wish they had, so consider yourself lucky in that regard! Give yourself permission to spend knowing that the money you've saved will continue to grow and be available to you as you need it.

Doing some retirement analysis

Understand the standard of living that can be provided by the assets you've already accumulated. There are numerous useful retirement planning analytic tools you can use to assess where you currently stand in terms of saving for retirement.

TIP

Among the various mass market website retirement tools, I really like T. Rowe Price's (www.troweprice.com/usis/advice/tools/retirement-income-calculator) and Vanguard's (investor.vanguard.com/calculator-tools/retirement-income-calculator/).

Getting smart about investing your money

While super savers love watching their money grow, some have trouble with investing in volatile wealth-building investments like stocks because they generally abhor losing money. Even bonds can be a turnoff because they, too, can fluctuate in value.

So, part of the challenge with getting comfortable with spending more of your money is to get wiser about investing. Please see Chapter 6.

Going on a news diet

Super savers often benefit from minimizing and even avoiding news programs that dwell on the negative, which only reinforces their fears about never having enough money. One justification that super savers use for their actions that constantly resurfaces in the news is the litany of fears surrounding the tens of millions of baby boomers hitting retirement age around the same time. The story goes that retiring boomers will cause a mammoth collapse of the stock market as they sell out to finance their golden years. Real-estate prices are supposed to plummet as well, as everyone sells their larger homes and retires to small condominiums in the Sun Belt.

Such doomsaying about the future of financial and real-estate markets is unfounded. The fear that boomers will suddenly sell everything when they hit retirement is bogus. Nobody sells off their entire nest egg the day after they stop working; retirement can last up to 30+ years, and assets are depleted quite gradually. On top of that, boomers vary in age by up to 16 years and, thus, will be retiring at different times. The wealthiest (who hold the bulk of real estate and stocks) won't even sell most of their holdings but will, like the wealthy of previous generations, pass on many of their assets.

Treating yourself to something special

Regularly buy something that you historically have viewed as frivolous but which you can truly afford. Once a week or once a month, treat yourself!

By all means, spend the money on something that brings you the most joy, whether it's eating out occasionally at a pricey restaurant or taking an extra vacation during the year. How about tickets to your favorite sporting events or other performances?

Buying more gifts for the people you love

Money hoarders actually tend to be more generous with loved ones than they are with themselves. However, over-savers still tend to squelch their desires to buy gifts or help out those they care about.

Think about those you care most about and what would bring joy to their lives. Try hard to think about what they really value and enjoy.

Going easy when it comes to everyday expenses

How would you like it if a family member or close friend followed you around all day and totaled up the number of calories that you consumed? Well, then, why would you expect your family to happily accept your daily, weekly, and monthly tracking of their expenditures? In some families, super savers who habitually track their spending drive others crazy with their perpetual money monitoring. Personal finances become a constant source of unnecessary stress and anxiety.

Especially if you're automatically saving money from each paycheck or saving on a monthly basis, does it really matter where the rest of it goes? (Of course, none of us wants family members to engage in illegal or harmful behaviors. But other than that, enjoy life.)

Work at establishing guidelines and a culture of spending money that everyone can agree and live with. Some couples, for example, only discuss larger purchases, which are defined as exceeding a certain dollar limit such as $100 or $200. Parents who teach their children about spending wisely pass along far more valuable financial lessons than do elders who nag and complain about specific purchases.

Chapter **8**

Estate Planning: Leaving a Legacy

lthough some of us don't like to admit or think about it, we are all mortal. Because of the way our legal and tax systems work, it's beneficial when people die to have legal documents in place specifying what should be done with assets and other important details. This chapter gets you started on the right foot.

Wills, Trusts, and Estate Planning

Estate planning is the process of determining what will happen to your assets after you die. Considering your mortality in the context of insurance may seem a bit odd. But the time and cost of various estate-planning maneuvers is really nothing more than buying insurance: You're ensuring that, after you die, everything will be taken care of as you wish, and taxes will be minimized. Thinking about estate planning in this way can help you better evaluate whether certain options make sense at particular points in your life.

Depending upon your circumstances, you may eventually want to contact an attorney who specializes in estate-planning matters. However, educating yourself first about the different options is worth your time. More than a few attorneys have their own agendas about what you should do, so be careful. And most of the estate-planning strategies that you're likely to benefit from don't require hiring an attorney.

Starting with a will

A will is the most basic of such documents, and for most people, particularly those who are younger or don't have great assets, the only critical one. Through a will, you can direct to whom your assets will go upon your death, as well as who will serve as guardian for your minor children.

In the absence of a will, state law dictates these important issues. Thus, your friends, less closely related relatives, and charities will likely receive nothing.

TIP

Also, make sure that your named beneficiaries on IRA accounts, for example, reflect your current wishes. Many people mistakenly believe that a will overrides their beneficiary statement or insurance.

Without a will, your heirs are powerless, and the state will appoint an administrator to supervise the distribution of your assets at a fee of around 5 percent of your estate. A bond must also be posted at a cost of hundreds of dollars.

In the event that both you and your spouse die without a will, the state (courts and social service agencies) will decide who will raise your children. Even if you cannot decide at this time who you want to raise your children, you should at least appoint a trusted guardian who can decide for you.

If you previously completed a will, how many years ago was it prepared, and have any significant changes happened in your life since then (for example, a move, the birth of a child, the passing of a named beneficiary, and so on)? If so, consider updating your will.

REMEMBER

A will isn't set in stone. You can change it over time as needed, so don't avoid making a will just because you haven't decided certain issues. If you're not sure about a few details, have a basic will prepared now and then change it as needed in future years.

Avoiding probate through living trusts

Because of the United States' quirky legal system, even if you have a will, some or all of your assets must go through a court process known as probate. *Probate* is the legal process for administering and implementing the directions in a will. Property and assets that are owned in joint tenancy or inside retirement accounts, such as IRAs or 401(k)s, generally pass to heirs without having to go through probate. However, most other assets are probated.

A *living trust* effectively transfers assets into a trust. As the trustee, you control those assets, and you can revoke the trust whenever you desire. The advantage of a living trust is that upon your death, assets can pass directly to your beneficiaries without going through probate. Probate can be a lengthy, expensive hassle for your heirs — with legal fees tallying 5 percent or more of the value of the estate. In addition, your assets become a matter of public record as a result of probate.

Living trusts are likely to be of greatest value to people who meet one or more of the following criteria (the more that apply, the more value trusts have):

- » Age 60 or older
- » Single
- » Assets worth more than $100,000 that must pass through probate (including real estate, nonretirement accounts, and small businesses)
- » Real property held in other states

As with a will, you do *not* need an attorney to establish a legal and valid living trust. Attorney fees for establishing a living trust can range from hundreds to thousands of dollars. Hiring an attorney is of greatest value to people with large estates (see the next section) who don't have the time, desire, and expertise to maximize the value derived from estate planning. Also consult with an attorney if you have nonstandard wishes to be carried out, such as special-needs beneficiaries or extra control measures you want applied to assets after incapacity or death.

Note: Living trusts keep assets out of probate but have nothing to do with minimizing estate or inheritance taxes.

Considering your preparation options

The simplest and lowest-cost way to prepare a will and living trust is to use one of the high-quality, user-friendly software packages developed by attorneys. You do not need an attorney to prepare a legal will and living trust. Most attorneys, in fact, have their administrative staff prepare wills using a software package! What makes a will valid is that it is witnessed by three people.

Nolo's online will (Nolo Press; store.nolo.com/products) is an excellent program for preparing wills as well as other standard legal documents (such as healthcare directives and durable powers of attorney for finances). Don't use "fill in the blank" will kits, which are prone to errors and challenge.

If doing it all yourself seems overwhelming, by all means hire an attorney. Be sure to retain the services of one who specializes in wills, trusts, and related issues. Also, don't be shy about questioning costs and doing some comparison shopping.

TIP

If preparing the will all by yourself seems overwhelming, you can (instead of hiring an attorney) use a paralegal typing service to help you prepare the documents. These services generally charge 50 percent or less of what an attorney charges.

Reducing estate taxes

Under current tax laws, an individual can pass $13.99 million to beneficiaries without having to pay federal estate taxes (married couples can pass $27.98 million).

Whether you should be concerned about possible estate taxes depends on several issues. How much of your assets you're going to use up during your life is the first and most important issue you need to consider. This amount depends on how much your assets grow over time, as well as how rapidly you spend money. During retirement, you'll (hopefully) be using at least some of your money.

I've seen too many affluent individuals, especially in their retirements, worry about estate taxes on their assets. Here are some actions you can take to reduce those taxes:

>> **Gifting:** You can give $19,000 annually to each of your beneficiaries, *tax-free*. By giving away money, you reduce

your estate and, therefore, the estate taxes owed on it. Any appreciation on the value of the gift between the date of the gift and your date of death is also out of your estate and not subject to estate taxes.

>> **Establish a bypass trust:** Although it's no longer generally necessary at the federal level, you may want to establish a *bypass trust* to effectively double the estate tax limit for your state. Upon the death of the first spouse, assets held in their name go into the bypass trust, effectively removing those assets from the remaining spouse's taxable estate. (Speak with an estate-planning attorney.)

>> **Cash value life insurance:** This type of life insurance is another estate-planning tool. Unfortunately, it's a tool that's overused or, I should say, oversold. People who sell cash value insurance — that is, insurance salespeople and others masquerading as financial planners — too often advocate life insurance as the one and only way to reduce estate taxes. Other methods for reducing estate taxes are usually superior, because they don't require wasting money on life insurance.

TIP

Small-business owners whose businesses are worth several million dollars or more may want to consider cash value life insurance under specialized circumstances. If you lack the necessary additional assets to pay expected estate taxes and you don't want your beneficiaries to be forced to sell the business, you can buy cash value life insurance to pay expected estate taxes.

To find out more about how to reduce your estate (and other) taxes, visit my website at www.erictyson.com.

Power of Attorney: Appointing Your Financial Sidekick

One of the most important documents in a good estate plan (other than a will, which I discuss in the preceding section) is the *financial power of attorney* (POA). This document designates someone (or several people) to take financial actions when you are unable. They can pay bills, change investments, and make other necessary moves. They even can make estate planning gifts, if you provide that in the document.

REMEMBER

Unlike the will, the financial power of attorney takes effect while you're alive but unable to act because of a temporary or permanent disability.

The POA is a document I hope you don't ever need, but like insurance, you need to prepare it ahead of time to ensure that you have it if you ever need to use it. The following sections look at why you need a POA and how you can choose the one that's right for you.

Recognizing the importance of a POA

Without the POA (or a living trust, which I discuss in the earlier section "Avoiding probate through living trusts"), your finances can't be managed without your approval. Any property solely in your name, including your business, legally can't be sold or managed by anyone else. Bills can't be paid, and your portfolio can't be managed. Loans can't be taken out against your assets.

REMEMBER

Joint ownership eliminates some, but not all, of these problems. With joint ownership of a checking account, the joint owner usually can write checks to pay bills. But joint owners of property generally can't sell assets or borrow against them, though the rules vary from state to state and also can be altered by a joint ownership agreement.

To manage your financial affairs when you're unable to and don't have a POA, your family must go to court and obtain an order stating that you're not competent to manage your affairs. This process takes time and money and can be very unpleasant for all involved. In addition, by drafting a POA, you determine who manages your finances. Without it, a court decides, and the person appointed may not be the one you would prefer to handle your financial affairs.

The person named in the POA to act on your behalf is known as an *agent* or an *attorney-in-fact*. This person legally may do in your name anything you can do. If you sign an unlimited power of attorney, the agent has authority to act in your name in all matters. Under a limited power of attorney, the agent has the power to act only on matters that you specify. You may revoke a POA any time you have legal capacity (such as when you aren't considered incapacitated).

Whether you choose an unlimited or a limited POA, you also want to sign a *durable power of attorney*. Under the durable POA, the document remains in effect even after you're incapacitated. A potential drawback to the durable POA is that it's valid as soon as you sign it — even though you aren't incapacitated. It's possible that an attorney-in-fact who isn't trustworthy could take actions at any time.

Some states recognize the *springing power of attorney*. Under the springing POA, the agent has power only after a disability occurs. A disadvantage to the springing power of attorney is that it must have a definition of disability and a process for having you declared incapacitated. These requirements can make the document less effective than the durable POA, and disagreements can lead to the same court action that the power of attorney was partly created to avoid. In addition, only a few states recognize it.

Choosing the right POA

Of course you want to carefully select your attorney-in-fact. Naming a spouse or adult child as the agent is tempting — and it may work well in many cases — but it can be risky if those folks don't have the same ideas about things as you do or aren't capable of managing your assets effectively.

Consider situations when more than bill paying is required. For example, if the stock market experiences a sharp decline while you're incapacitated, do you want someone who's going to panic and sell all your depressed investments or do you want someone who will adhere to your long-term plan? Choose someone who can judge when to change a long-term plan and when to stick with it.

In selecting a POA, you want someone who's trusted and reliable. You also want someone who's likely to be around and have the time to take on the position when needed. The person should understand your views and philosophy on managing your finances and have good judgment on financial matters. You may have a simple estate and require someone who's simply organized and reliable to pay bills. Or you may have a complicated estate and need someone who's fairly sophisticated or at least wise enough to consult with your advisors and make good decisions.

REMEMBER

Be sure to name at least one alternate attorney-in-fact, because something could happen to the original designee. You can even name more than one attorney-in-fact and require them to act jointly. Doing so protects against both fraud and bad judgment. It also means they have to be located near each other and meet regularly. These requirements could impede decision making.

After you select your POA, you'll likely have to prepare and sign many documents. Consider the following:

>> Most financial services companies have their own forms and will accept only their forms when someone asserts a power of attorney. They also want copies of the form on file before you're disabled.

>> When you live in more than one state, you may need to provide a different document for each state.

TIP

Review the POA as part of your regular estate plan assessment. Consider whether the attorney-in-fact is still the best choice, and review the scope of the powers. When you open new financial accounts, make sure that the account custodians have copies of the POA documentation they will accept.

Advanced Directives: Making Medical Decisions Ahead of Time

Most of your estate plan concerns money, property, and other financial issues. But it's generally accepted that a complete estate plan should have at least one nonfinancial document. You should have a financial power of attorney empowering someone to manage your finances when you can't. But, you also need one or more documents to cover decisions about your medical care when you're unable to make such decisions.

An essential document is the *medical care directive*. When creating this document, make sure that you prepare multiple versions if you travel regularly to other states. You want to make sure that the documents are enforceable in those states as well as in your home state.

Several different types of medical directive documents are available. You need to understand their differences and decide which are right for you. That's where this section comes into play.

A good estate planning attorney will include these in your plan. Software that helps prepare wills usually has these documents, too. Many states have official versions authorized by law and have sample versions available on their websites, usually under the Department of Health or a similar agency. You also can locate these and other forms through www.agingwithdignity.org. I don't endorse all the statements and philosophies on this site. I refer to them only as a place to find sample documents. As always, you'll find many nuances in these documents, so it's safest to have an estate planning attorney prepare them.

Understanding living wills

The *living will* (called a *healthcare proxy* in some states) is the best-known medical directive document. This type of will states that in certain circumstances you either want or don't want certain types of care. The most basic living will states:

> "If I have a terminal condition, and there is no hope of recovery, I do not want my life prolonged by artificial means."

Some living wills span many pages, prescribing the treatment to use or not use in different situations. Creating a living will is simple. Most states recognize living wills and even have authorized sample forms available on their websites.

Despite its popularity, the living will has some important disadvantages you need to be aware of:

>> **Applying the living will's simple principles can be difficult in real-world situations.** Medical professionals, for example, may disagree over whether you have any hope of improvement. But even when the experts agree, your family members may disagree. If a person's living will prohibits artificial means of life support, there may be disagreement over whether maintenance care (such as feeding and hydration tubes) is considered artificial life support.

>> **Adding specific details to a custom living will doesn't eliminate all problems.** Even detailed documents can't cover all possible scenarios, leaving decision-makers uncertain of what to do. Also, technology and medical knowledge change. Conditions that couldn't be treated a few years ago can be treated now. Also, people may disagree

over the facts, such as the diagnosis, probability of improvement, and whether a person is in a vegetative state.

>> **Perhaps most important, in many cases, living wills simply aren't effective.** Studies reveal that medical professionals often don't see the documents until after treatment decisions are made. Some ignore the documents or interpret them differently than what you intended, because they fear surviving family members will sue for failure to treat. In addition, a doctor can interpret a document to approve treatment in a circumstance when others interpret it to withhold treatment. Even when a doctor believes the living will prescribes nontreatment in a situation, treatment still is likely to be given if one or more key family members request it.

REMEMBER

Some people disparage living wills because of these drawbacks. Others say these disadvantages are relatively rare occurrences. Because of the uneven performance of living wills, you shouldn't rely solely on them. Despite their imperfections, the family discussions prompted in advance by the crafting of a living will makes them worthwhile in my view. Instead, your estate plan should include more than one medical care document. The following sections discuss additional documents to consider. Some estate planning attorneys prepare all these documents as part of their clients' plans.

Signing DNRs

A simple document called the *do not resuscitate* (DNR) or *do not hospitalize* (DNH) order can be helpful for delegating medical decisions. DNR and DNH orders state that the person isn't to be resuscitated (such as by using CPR) or hospitalized. These documents are becoming common among much older people who are frail, especially those in nursing homes.

Some people sign these documents because they believe additional treatment for new ailments or developments won't prolong their lives or improve their quality of life. They decline CPR or hospitalization (or both) in advance, instead opting to be kept comfortable in their residences. Advocates of the orders say CPR rarely helps these individuals recover and often makes their deaths violent and painful.

DNR and DNH documents need to be kept in your medical chart with each of your care providers, and any medical personnel who treat you regularly should be made aware of them.

Assigning a healthcare proxy or POA

The *healthcare proxy* or *healthcare power of attorney* document appoints one or more people to make medical decisions when you're unable. This document is similar to the financial power of attorney. The healthcare POA should be in every estate plan.

With the healthcare POA, the agents discuss your situation with your medical providers and make a treatment decision. You may use the other medical care directive documents in this chapter as statements of your wishes to guide the decision-makers. (In the living will and DNR/DNH orders, you state the care you want or don't want in certain situations. With those documents, you try to make decisions in advance, though you won't know what all the facts and circumstances will be.)

Naming more than one proxy or agent may be a good idea because it takes some of the responsibility off of one person and may ensure a more complete consideration of all the factors. When more than one person is appointed, you may want to require that all agree before treatment can be withheld or given. Some people appoint only family members; others believe at least one proxy should be a person who knows the family but isn't a part of it.

The people you appoint as healthcare POAs must be likely to be available when medical decisions are needed. Someone who doesn't live nearby, travels a lot, or generally isn't easy to get in touch with may not be a good choice.

Authorizing HIPAA

This document authorizes medical providers to release information to the named persons without violating the privacy provisions of the Health Insurance Portability and Accountability Act of 1996. Without this document, medical professionals won't generally share information about your medical situation even with your family members or holders of POAs.

Combining documents

One estate planning innovation is to combine all the medical care directive documents that I discuss in this chapter into one called an *advanced healthcare directive.*

In addition to combining the living will and healthcare power of attorney, the directive can include more detailed explanations of your philosophy and preferences in different situations. The document also can include information such as how you want to be made comfortable and be treated as well as other non-medical decisions. Some directives even have instructions regarding music, grooming, fresh flowers, and other aspects of your environment while receiving care.

TIP

Sample all-in-one documents are available as a package titled Five Wishes from Aging with Dignity. Go to www.agingwith dignity.org, or call 888-5-WISHES (888- 594-7437). The organization charges modest fees for the documents and has versions for most states.

IN THIS CHAPTER

» Making good decisions during a
   financial crisis

» Adapting your financial approach during
   life changes

» Adopting proven strategies during times
   of upheaval

Chapter 9

Staying Financially Resilient in a Volatile World

M anaging your money involves making decisions that will carry you through times of economic downturns as well as personal crises and life changes. Although every crisis is unique and may affect you differently, the advice I offer in this chapter represents some of the best ways I know to stay afloat financially and emotionally.

Riding Economic Ups and Downs Without Losing Your Hat

When a major crisis hits — for example, the 2008 financial crisis and lengthy recession, the 2020 COVID-19 pandemic, the 2001 terrorist attacks and associated recession — unexpected things happen. And if you're one of the millions of people adversely affected, stress and emotions can add to the financial quandaries and problems you face. Each crisis is unique and impacts the economy and individuals personally in differing ways.

Past experience and the "school of hard knocks" can certainly improve how well you react to each such event. But you can prepare for and better manage through especially challenging times by examining such past episodes and following the strategies that I describe in this section.

Examine the missteps of others

You probably didn't know or realize it at the time, but the 2008 financial crisis actually shared numerous parallels with the so-called Panic of 1907. And the 1907 panic was similar to other financial panics, bank runs, and bank failures that came before it. Such episodes were reasonably common as the government-operated Federal Deposit Insurance Corporation (FDIC) insurance system for banks didn't come into existence until 1933. There was also no other federal oversight or backstop for banks, like the Federal Reserve, which didn't exist in 1907 (but came out of this crisis).

Plenty of folks were worried about the safety of their money with the stock and real-estate markets getting pummeled during the 2008 financial crisis. But folks worrying about the safety of keeping their money in the bank reflected irrational fear. If the FDIC government system backing up our banking system failed to protect bank account depositors, holding onto paper money, also issued by the U.S. federal government, wouldn't do you any good either.

Most folks can see the silliness and danger of keeping cash in a cracker box in your home. Cash kept in your home can be stolen, forgotten, or destroyed in a fire. Hearing stories like this can lull us into thinking that, well, we would never do something so ill-advised, yet many people make decisions and take actions that are nearly certain to lead to suboptimal or even terrible outcomes.

TIP

Make a point of studying economic history. Understand which strategies worked — and which did not work (and why) — during times of economic and financial market downs. Consider what has changed between the past and present (such as the introduction of the FDIC insurance system for banks) that may inform taking different actions. You can read much more about U.S. economic history in *Financial Security For Dummies* (authored by yours truly and published by Wiley).

Avoid common mistakes

The following are some of the detrimental financial moves I have seen people make during economic and financial market calamities. Avoid making these mistakes:

>> **Selling stocks at greatly reduced/depressed prices:** When stocks are falling in value fast and the daily news is filled with gloomy headlines about job losses and other economic problems, I've seen plenty of otherwise intelligent folks dump their stocks and buy bonds or simply sit on cash in a money market or bank account. Typically, during such episodes, bonds are in high demand (and thus at elevated prices) and offering reduced yields. Now, don't get me wrong — I understand the emotions behind this. No one enjoys feeling like they're going down with a sinking ship or part of the losing team. But selling stocks low and buying bonds high is the opposite of how smart investors make money. Otherwise-sound investments that are beaten down in price offer value. That's why smart long-term investors buy, not sell, stocks after they've fallen, and you should as well.

>> **Following supposed prognosticators who claim to have predicted all these bad things that have recently happened:** Fibbing and misrepresentation are rampant on social media platforms. And the mainstream media should really do a much better job vetting people they are giving airtime to. Sure, sometimes a pundit gets something right in the short term, but what about their longer-term track record and how accurate or not that was?

>> **Heeding misinformation and uninformed people on social media platforms and blogs:** For example, in response to a 2008 news report about housing prices dropping significantly from the prior year, consider this online posting, "Even if there were mortgages to be had, people have learned a valuable lesson from this housing bubble. No one in their right mind is buying now unless they're looking at at least a 50 percent discount . . . from today's prices!" If you were already stressed about challenging economic times, reading such gibberish would just make you more anxious. The reality was that there were plenty of mortgages being done then, and real-estate prices weren't

going to (and didn't) fall 50 percent from those depressed levels.

>> **Immersing yourself in excessive and negative short-term news:** When a crisis is unfolding, of course you're going to want to keep up with what's happening. The problem, however, comes from the fact that news (and opinions) come at us 24/7 now, and so much of it is geared toward sensationalism and raising your anxieties to keep you tuned in. The "news" almost always focuses on the very short term and fails to provide a long-term perspective. The more you consume, the more stressed and depressed you are likely to become and the more likely you are to make emotionally based moves that are detrimental to your long-term interests.

>> **Listening to politicians.** Even when there isn't a crisis or major economic problem, many politicians make things sound dire, especially when the other party is in power/control or we're coming out of an event for which they blame the other side.

Embrace financial strategies that work

REMEMBER

Keep these strategies in mind as you manage your money in the years ahead:

>> **Hold onto your long-term investments like stocks and real estate during downturns.** It's impossible to know how long and deep a downturn will be, and history has shown that prices can bounce back quickly, so you're not going to be able to time buying back well if you try to exit and miss a part of the decline.

>> **Read and review news and other sources that help you maintain balance and a long-term perspective.** This likely means limiting your diet of daily news and choosing your resources carefully.

>> **Take advantage of depressed investing prices:** Consider using extra cash to take advantage of depressed investing prices to buy more at favorable prices.

>> **Don't beat yourself up for past mistakes.** Everyone makes mistakes. Wise people learn and grow from their mistakes.

Adopt a positive mindset

Be prepared for times of economic hardship by adopting a positive mindset. Here are some strategies that work:

>> **Stay in financial shape.** An athlete is best able to withstand physical adversities during competition by prior training and eating well. Likewise, the sounder your finances are to begin with, the better you'll be able to deal with life changes.

>> **Remember that changes require change.** Even if your financial house is in order, a major life change — starting a family, buying a home, starting a business, divorcing, retiring — should prompt you to review your personal financial strategies. Life changes affect your income, spending, insurance needs, and ability to take financial risk.

>> **Don't procrastinate.** With a major life change on the horizon, procrastination can be costly. You (and your family) may overspend and accumulate high-cost debts, lack proper insurance coverage, or take other unnecessary risks. Early preparation can save you from these pitfalls.

>> **Manage stress and your emotions.** Life changes often are accompanied by stress and other emotional upheavals. Don't make snap decisions during these changes. Take the time to become fully informed and recognize and acknowledge your feelings. Educating yourself is key. You may want to hire experts to help but don't abdicate decisions and responsibilities to advisors — the advisors may not have your best interests at heart or fully appreciate your needs.

Adaptability: The Financial Chameleon's Superpower

Some of life's changes come unexpectedly, like earthquakes. Others you can see coming when they're still far off, like the birth of a child. Whether a life change is predictable or not, your ability to navigate successfully through its challenges and adjust to new circumstances depends largely on your degree of preparedness.

Here, then, are some of the major changes you may anticipate in your life and strategies to prepare for them. Chapter 2 covers unexpected events that you may have to deal with. Of course, I wish you more of the good changes than the bad.

Starting out: Your first job

If you just graduated from college or some other program, or you're otherwise entering the workforce, your increased income and reduction in educational expenses are probably a welcome relief. You'd think, then, that more young adults would be able to avoid financial trouble. But they face challenges because of poor financial habits picked up at home or from the world at large. Here's how to get on the path to financial success:

>> **Use credit cards responsibly.** While this point may seem obvious, so many people do not use credit cards appropriately. Be sure that you are charging only what you can pay off each month. Set up automatic electronic payment from your bank/investment account to help you make sure that you are paying off the full amount each month. Don't use a credit card to borrow money to buy something you can't afford.

If you have trouble keeping yourself in check with a credit card, try using a debit card (see Chapter 3) instead.

>> **Get in the habit of saving and investing.** Ideally, your savings should be directed into retirement accounts that offer tax benefits, unless you want to accumulate down-payment money for other goals such as a home or small-business purchase (see Chapter 7). Thinking about a home purchase or retirement is usually not in the active thought patterns of first-time job seekers. I'm often asked, "At what age should a person start saving?" To me, that's similar to asking at what age you should start brushing your teeth. Well, when you have teeth to brush! So I say you should start saving and investing money from your first paycheck. Try saving 5 percent of every paycheck and then eventually increase your savings to 10 percent. If you're having trouble saving money, track your spending and make cutbacks as needed (see Chapter 3).

>> **Get insured.** When you're young and healthy, imagining yourself feeling otherwise is hard. Many twenty-somethings give little thought to the potential for healthcare expenses.

But because accidents and unexpected illnesses can strike at any age, forgoing coverage can be financially devastating. When you're in your first full-time job with more-limited benefits, buying disability coverage, which replaces income lost due to a long-term disability, is also wise. And as you begin to build your assets, consider making out a will so that your assets go where you want them to in the event of your untimely passing. Chapter 4 covers insurance.

>> **Continue your education.** After you get out in the workforce, you (like many other people) may realize how little you learned in formal schooling that can actually be used in the real world, and conversely, how much you need to learn that school never taught you. Read, learn, and continue to grow. The best books, blogs, podcasts, seminars, and mentorships are but a few of the ways to learn and grow. Continuing education can help you advance in your career and enjoy the world around you.

Changing jobs or careers

During your adult life, you'll almost surely change jobs — perhaps several times a decade. I hope that most of the time you'll be changing by your own choice. But let's face it: Downsizing has impacted even the most talented workers, and more industries are subjected to global competition.

TIP

Always be prepared for a job change. No matter how happy you are in your current job, knowing that your world won't fall apart if you're not working tomorrow can give you an added sense of security and encourage openness to possibility. Whether you're changing your job by choice or necessity, the following financial maneuvers can help ease the transition:

>> **Structure your finances to afford an income dip.** Spending less than you earn always makes good financial sense, but if you're approaching a possible job change, spending less is even more important, particularly if you're entering a new field, facing a period of unemployment, or starting your own company and you expect a short-term income dip. Many people view a lifestyle of thriftiness as restrictive, but ultimately those thrifty habits can give you more freedom to do what you want to do. Be sure to keep an emergency reserve fund (see Chapter 2).

If you lose your job, batten down the hatches. You normally get little advance warning when you lose your job through no choice of your own. It doesn't mean, however, that you can't do anything financially. Evaluating and slashing your current level of spending may be necessary. Everything should be fair game, from how much you spend on housing to how often you eat out to where you do your grocery shopping. Avoid at all costs the temptation to maintain your level of spending by accumulating consumer debt.

>> **Evaluate the total financial picture when relocating.** At some point in your career, you may have the option of relocating. But don't call the moving company until you understand the financial consequences of such a move. You can't simply compare salaries and benefits between the two jobs. You also should compare the cost of living between the two areas: housing, commuting, state income and property taxes, food, utilities, and all other major expenditure categories.

Getting married

Ready to tie the knot with the one you love? Congratulations — I hope that you'll have a long, healthy, and happy life together. In addition to the emotional and moral commitments that you and your spouse will make to one another, you're probably going to be merging many of your financial decisions and resources. Even if you're largely in agreement about your financial goals and strategies, managing as two is far different than managing as one. Here's how to prepare:

>> **Take a compatibility test.** Many couples talk too little about their goals and plans before marriage, and failing to do so breaks up marriages. Finances are just one of numerous issues you should discuss. Ensuring that you know what you're getting yourself into is a good way to minimize your chances for heartache. Ministers, priests, and rabbis sometimes offer premarital counseling to help bring issues and differences to the surface.

>> **Discuss and set joint goals.** After you're married, you and your spouse should set aside time once a year, or every few years, to discuss personal and financial goals for the years ahead. When you talk about where you want to go, you help ensure that you're both rowing your financial boat in unison.

>> **Decide whether to keep finances separate or manage them jointly.** Philosophically, I like the idea of pooling your finances better. After all, marriage is a partnership. In some marriages, however, spouses choose to keep some money separate so that they don't feel the scrutiny of a spouse with different spending preferences. Spouses who have been through divorce may choose to keep the assets they bring into the new marriage separate in order to protect their money in the event of another divorce. As long as you're jointly accomplishing what you need to financially, some separation of money is okay. But for the health of your marriage, don't hide money, transactions (unless it's a gift for your spouse), or debts from one another, and if you're the higher-income spouse, don't assume power and control over your joint income.

TIP

>> **Coordinate and maximize employer benefits.** If one or both of you have access to a package of employee benefits through an employer, understand how best to make use of those benefits. Coordinating and using the best that each package has to offer is like getting a pay raise. If you both have access to health insurance, compare plans to determine which of you has better benefits. Likewise, one of you may have a better retirement savings plan — one that matches and offers superior investment options. Unless you can afford to save the maximum through both your plans, saving more in the better plan will increase your combined assets. (*Note:* If you're concerned about what will happen if you save more in one of your retirement plans and then you divorce, in most states, the money is considered part of your joint assets to be divided equally.)

>> **Discuss life and disability insurance needs.** If you and your spouse can make do without each other's income, you may not need any income-protecting insurance. However, if you both depend on each other's incomes, or if one of you depends fully or partly on the other's income, you may each need long-term disability and term life insurance policies (see Chapter 4).

>> **Update your wills.** When you marry, you should make or update your wills. Having a will is potentially more valuable when you're married, especially if you want to leave money to others in addition to your spouse, or if you have children for whom you need to name a guardian. See Chapter 8 for more on wills.

>> **Reconsider beneficiaries on investment and life insurance.** With retirement accounts and life insurance policies, you name beneficiaries to whom the money or value in those accounts will go in the event of your passing. When you marry, you'll probably want to revisit and rethink your beneficiaries.

Buying a home

Most Americans eventually buy a home. You don't need to own a home to be a financial success, but homeownership certainly offers financial rewards. Over the course of your adult life, the real estate you own is likely going to appreciate in value. Additionally, you'll pay off your mortgage someday, which will greatly reduce your housing costs. If you're thinking about buying a home, take these steps:

>> **Get your overall finances in order.** Before buying, analyze your current budget, your ability to afford debt, and your future financial goals. Make sure that your expected housing expenses allow you to save properly for retirement and other long- or short-term objectives. Don't buy a home based on the maximum amount lenders are willing to lend you.

>> **Determine whether now's the time.** Buying a house when you don't see yourself staying put for three to five years rarely makes financial sense. Buying and selling a home gobbles up a good deal of money in transaction costs — you'll be lucky to recoup all those costs even within a five-year period. Also, if your income is likely to drop or you have other pressing goals, such as starting a business, you may want to wait to buy.

Having children

If you think that being a responsible adult, holding down a job, paying your bills on time, and preparing for your financial future are tough, wait 'til you add kids to the mix. Most parents find that with children in the family, their already precious free time and money become much scarcer. The sooner you discover how to manage your time and money, the better able you'll be to have a sane, happy, and financially successful life as a parent. Here are some key things to do both before and after you begin your family:

>> **Set your priorities.** As with many other financial decisions, starting or expanding a family requires that you plan ahead. Set your priorities and structure your finances and living situation accordingly. Is having a bigger home in a particular community important, or would you rather feel less pressure to work hard, giving you more time to spend with your family? Keep in mind that a less hectic work life not only gives you more free time but also often reduces your cost of living by decreasing meals out, dry-cleaning costs, day care expenses, and so on.

>> **Take a hard look at your budget.** Having kids requires you to increase your spending. At a minimum, expenditures for food and clothing will increase. But you're also likely to spend more on housing, insurance, day care, and education. On top of that, if you want to play an active role in raising your children, working at some full-time jobs may not be possible. So while you consider the added expenses, you may also need to factor in a decrease in income.

No simple rules exist for estimating how kids will affect your household's income and expenses. On the income side, figure out how much you want to cut back on work. On the expense side, government statistics show that the average household with school-age children spends about 20 percent more than a household without children. Going through your budget category by category and estimating how kids will change your spending is a more scientific approach.

>> **Boost insurance coverage *before* getting pregnant.** Make sure you have health insurance in place if you're going to try to get pregnant. Even though the Affordable Care Act mandated maternity benefits in all health plans, if you lack coverage and then get pregnant, you won't be able to enroll outside of the small portion of the year for open enrollment. With disability insurance, pregnancy is considered a preexisting condition, so women should secure this coverage before getting pregnant. And most families-to-be should buy life insurance. Buying life insurance *after* the bundle of joy comes home from the hospital is a risky proposition — if one of the parents develops a health problem, they may be denied coverage. You should also consider buying life insurance for a stay-at-home parent. Even though the stay-at-home parent is not bringing in income, if they were to pass away, hiring assistance could harm the family budget.

- » **Check maternity leave with your employers.** Many of the larger employers offer some maternity leave for women, and in increasing cases, for men. Some employers offer paid leaves, while others may offer unpaid leaves. Understand the options and the financial ramifications before you consider the leave and, ideally, before you get pregnant. Also, check laws within your state for mandated maternity and paternity leave.

- » **Update your will.** If you have a will, update it; if you don't have a will, make one now. With children in the picture, you need to name a guardian who will be responsible for raising your children should you and your spouse both pass away.

- » **Enroll the baby in your health plan.** After you welcome your baby into this world, enroll your newborn in your health insurance plan. Most insurers give you about a month or so to enroll.

- » **Understand child-care tax benefits.** You may be eligible for a $2,000 tax credit for each child under the age of 17. That should certainly motivate you to apply for your kid's Social Security number!

  If you and your spouse both work and you have children under the age of 13 or a disabled dependent of any age, you can also claim a tax credit for child-care expenses. The tax credit may be for up to 35 percent to a maximum of $3,000 in qualifying expenses for one child or dependent, or up to $6,000 for two or more children or dependents. Or you may work for an employer who offers a flexible benefit or spending plan. These plans allow you to put away up to $5,000 per year on a pre-tax basis for child-care expenses. For many parents, especially those in higher income tax brackets, these plans can save a lot in taxes. Keep in mind, however, that if you use one of these plans, you can't claim the child-care tax credit. Also, if you don't deplete the account every tax year, you forfeit any money left over.

WARNING

- » **Skip saving in custodial accounts.** One common concern is how to sock away enough money to pay for the ever-rising cost of a college education. If you start saving money in your child's name in a so-called custodial account, however, you may harm your family's future ability to qualify for financial aid (reduced college pricing) and miss out on the tax benefits that come with investing elsewhere.

>> **Don't indulge the children.** Toys, art classes, music lessons, travel sports and associated lessons, smartphones, field trips, and the like can rack up big bills, especially if you don't control your spending. Some parents fail to set guidelines or limits when spending on children's programs. Others foolishly follow the examples set by the families of their children's peers. Introspective parents have told me that they feel some insecurity about providing the best for their children. The parents (and kids) who seem the happiest and most financially successful are the ones who clearly distinguish between material luxuries and family necessities.

As children get older and become indoctrinated into the world of shopping, all sorts of other purchases come into play. Consider giving your kids a weekly allowance and letting them discover how to spend and manage it. And when they're old enough, having your kids get a part-time job can help teach financial responsibility.

Starting a small business

Many people aspire to be their own bosses, but far fewer people actually leave their jobs in order to achieve that dream. Giving up the apparent security of a job with benefits and a built-in network of co-workers is difficult for most people, both psychologically and financially. Starting a small business is not for everyone, but don't let inertia stand in your way. Here are some tips to help get you started and increase your chances for long-term success:

>> **Prepare to ditch your job.** To maximize your ability to save money, live as Spartan a lifestyle as you can while you're employed; you'll develop thrifty habits that'll help you weather the reduced income and increased expenditure period that comes with most small-business start-ups. You may also want to consider easing into your small business by working at it part time in the beginning, with or without cutting back on your normal job.

>> **Develop a business plan.** If you research and think through your business idea, not only will you reduce the likelihood of your business failing and increase its success if it thrives, but you'll also feel more comfortable taking the entrepreneurial plunge. A good business plan describes in detail the business

idea, the marketplace you'll compete in, your marketing plans, and expected revenue and expenses.

TIP

A good return on your tax dollars is utilizing the services of Small Business Development Centers (SBDC), which are nationwide. They will assist you with your business plan and loan packages for the Small Business Administration (SBA). Visit https://americassbdc.org for more information.

>> **Replace your insurance coverage.** Before you finally leave your job, get proper insurance. With health insurance, employers allow you to continue your existing coverage (at your own expense) for 18 months. For disability insurance, secure coverage before you leave your job so that you have income to qualify for coverage. If you have life insurance through your employer, obtain new individual coverage as soon as you know you're going to leave your job. (See Chapter 4 for details.)

>> **Establish a retirement savings plan.** After your business starts making a profit, consider establishing a retirement savings plan such as a SEP-IRA. Such plans allow you to shelter up to 20 percent of your business income from federal and state taxation.

Receiving a windfall

Whether through inheritance, stock options, small-business success, or lottery winnings, you may receive a financial windfall at some point in your life. Like many people who are totally unprepared psychologically and organizationally for their sudden good fortune, you may find that a flood of money can create more problems than it solves. Here are a few tips to help you make the most of your financial windfall:

>> **Educate yourself.** If you've never had to deal with significant wealth, I don't expect you to know how to handle it. Don't pressure yourself to invest it as soon as possible. Leaving the money where it is or stashing it in a higher-yielding money-market fund is far better than jumping into investments that you don't understand and haven't researched.

>> **Beware of the sharks.** You may begin to wonder whether someone has posted your net worth, address, and phone number in the local newspaper and on the internet. Brokers

WARNING

and financial advisors may flood you with marketing materials, telephone solicitations, and lunch date requests. These folks pursue you for a reason: They want to convert your money into their income either by selling you investments and other financial products or by managing your money. Stay away from the sharks, educate yourself, and take charge of your own financial moves. Decide on your own terms whom to hire and then seek them out.

>> **Recognize the emotional side of coming into a lot of money.** One of the side effects of accumulating wealth quickly is that you may have feelings of guilt or otherwise be unhappy, especially if you expected money to solve your problems. If you didn't invest in your relationship with your parents and, after their passing, you regret how you interacted with them, getting a big inheritance from your folks may make you feel bad. If you poured endless hours into a business venture that finally paid off, all that money in your investment accounts may leave you with a hollow feeling if you're divorced and you lost friends by neglecting your relationships.

>> **Pay down debts.** People generally borrow money to buy things that they otherwise can't buy in one fell swoop. Paying off your debts is one of the simplest and best investments you can make when you come into wealth.

>> **Diversify.** If you want to protect your wealth, don't keep it all in one pot. Mutual funds and exchange-traded funds (see Chapter 6) are ideally diversified, professionally managed investment vehicles to consider. And if you want your money to continue growing, consider wealth-building investments such as stocks, real estate, and small-business options.

>> **Make use of the opportunity.** Most people work for a paycheck for many decades so that they can pay a never-ending stream of monthly bills. Although I'm not advocating a hedonistic lifestyle, why not take some extra time to travel, spend time with your family, and enjoy the hobbies you've long been putting off? How about trying a new career that you may find more fulfilling and that may make the world a better place? And what about donating some to your favorite charities?

Retiring

If you've spent the bulk of your adult life working, retiring can be a challenging transition. Most Americans have an idealized vision of how wonderful retirement will be — no more irritating bosses and pressure of work deadlines; unlimited time to travel, play, and lead the good life. Sounds good, huh? Well, the reality for most Americans is different, especially for those who don't plan ahead (financially and otherwise). Here are some tips to help you through retirement:

REMEMBER

>> **Plan both financially and personally.** Planning your activities is even more important than planning financially. If the focus during your working years is solely on your career and saving money, you may lack interests, friends, and the ability to know how to spend money when you retire.

>> **Take stock of your resources.** Many people worry and wonder whether they have sufficient assets for cutting back on work or retiring completely, yet they don't crunch any numbers to see where they stand. Ignorance may cause you to misunderstand how little or how much you really have for retirement when compared to what you need.

>> **Reevaluate your insurance needs.** When you have sufficient assets to retire, you don't need to retain insurance to protect your employment income any longer. On the other hand, as your assets grow over the years, you may be underinsured with regards to liability insurance (see Chapter 4).

>> **Evaluate healthcare/living options.** Medical expenses in your retirement years (particularly the cost of nursing home care) can be daunting. Which course of action you take — supplemental insurance, buying into a retirement community, or not doing anything — depends on your financial and personal situation. Early preparation increases your options; if you wait until you have major health problems, it may be too late to choose specific paths.

>> **Decide what to do with your retirement plan money.** If you have money in a retirement savings plan, your employer may offer you the option of leaving the money in the plan rather than rolling it over into your own retirement account.

Brokers and financial advisors clearly prefer that you do the latter because it means more money for them, but it can also give you many more (and perhaps better) investment choices to consider.

>> **Pick a pension option.** Selecting a *pension option* (a plan that pays a monthly benefit during retirement) is similar to choosing a good investment — each pension option carries different risks, benefits, and tax consequences. Actuaries who base pension options on reasonable life expectancies structure pensions. The younger you are when you start collecting your pension, the less you get per month. Check to see whether the amount of your monthly pension stops increasing past a certain age. You obviously don't want to delay access to your pension benefits past that age, because you won't receive a reward for waiting any longer and you'll collect the benefit for fewer months.

If you know you have a health problem that shortens your life expectancy, you may benefit from drawing your pension sooner. If you plan to continue working in some capacity and earning a decent income after retiring, waiting for higher pension benefits when you're in a lower tax bracket is probably wise.

If you're married, consider how you want to structure survivorship options. At one end of the spectrum, you have the risky single life option, which pays benefits until you pass away and then provides no benefits for your spouse thereafter. This option maximizes your monthly take while you're alive. Consider this option only if your spouse can do without this income. The least risky option, and thus least financially rewarding while the pensioner is still living, is the *100-percent joint and survivor option,* which pays your survivor the same amount that you received while still alive. The other joint and survivor options fall somewhere between these two extremes and generally make sense for most couples who desire decent pensions early in retirement but want a reasonable amount to continue in the event that the pensioner dies first. The 75-percent joint and survivor option is a popular choice, because it closely matches the lower expense needs of the lone surviving spouse at 75 percent of the expenses of the couple, and it provides higher payments than the 100-percent joint and survivor option while both spouses are alive.

>> **Get your estate in order.** Confronting your mortality is never fun, but when you're considering retirement or you've already retired, getting your estate in order makes all the more sense. Find out about wills and trusts that may benefit you and your heirs. You may also want to consider giving monetary gifts now if you have more than you need. Doing so enables you to enjoy and see how others will utilize your funds.

Chapter **10**

Continuing Your Financial Education

We have too many options for finding "financial content" — radio and television news, websites, social media, podcasts, books, newspapers, and magazines that talk about money and purport to help you get rich. Tuning out poor resources and focusing on the best ones are the real challenges.

Because you probably don't consider yourself a financial expert, more often than not you may not know who to believe and listen to. I help you solve that problem in this chapter.

Identifying Reliable Sources of Financial Information

Over the years, money issues have received increased coverage through the major media of television, radio, and podcasts. Some topics gain more coverage because they help draw more advertising dollars (which follow what people are watching). When you tune into such programming, you generally don't pay a fee to tune in to a particular channel (with pay cable channels, streaming services, and satellite radio being exceptions). Advertising doesn't necessarily prevent a medium from delivering coverage that is objective and in your best interests, but it sure doesn't help foster this type of coverage either.

For example, can you imagine a financial radio or TV correspondent saying the following?

> *"We've decided to stop providing financial market updates every five minutes because we've found it causes some investors to become addicted to tracking the short-term movements in the markets and to lose sight of the bigger picture. We don't want to encourage people to make knee-jerk reactions to short-term events."*

Sound-bite-itis is another problem with much of the mass media. Producers and network executives believe that if you go into too much detail, viewers and listeners will change the channel.

Finding the best websites

Yes, the internet has changed the world, but certainly not always for the better and not always in such a big way. Consider the way we shop. You can buy things online that you couldn't in the past. Purchasing items online broadens the avenues through which you can spend money. I see a big downside here: Overspending is easier to do when you surf the internet a lot.

WARNING

Some of the best websites allow you to more efficiently access information that may help you make important investing decisions. However, this doesn't mean that your computer allows you to compete at the same level as professional money managers. The best pros work at their craft full time and have far more expertise and experience than the rest of us. Some nonprofessionals have been fooled into believing that investing online makes them better investors. My experience has been that people who spend time online daily dealing with investments tend to trade and react more to short-term events and have a harder time keeping the bigger picture and their long-term goals and needs in focus.

If you know where to look, you can more easily access some types of information. However, you often find a lot of garbage online — just as you do on other advertiser-dominated media like TV and radio. Those who navigate the internet and naively think that what's out there is useful "information," "research," or "objective advice," are in for a rude awakening.

Most personal finance sites on the internet are free, which — guess what — means that these sites are basically advertising or are dominated and driven by advertising. If you're looking for material written by unbiased experts or writers, finding it on the web may seem like searching for the proverbial needle in the haystack because the vast majority of what's online is biased and uninformed.

Considering the source so you can recognize bias

A report on the internet published by a leading investment-banking firm provides a list of the "coolest finance" sites. On the list is the website of a major bank. Because it has been a long time since I was in junior high school, I'm not quite sure what "cool" means anymore. If cool can be used to describe a well-organized and graphically pleasing website, then I guess I can say that the bank's site is cool.

However, if you're looking for sound information and advice, then the bank's site is decidedly "uncool." It steers you in a financial direction that benefits (not surprisingly) the bank and not you. For example, in the real-estate section, users are asked to plug in their gross monthly income and down payment. The information is then used to spit out the supposed amount that users can "afford" to spend on a home. No mention is given to the other financial goals and concerns — such as saving for retirement — that affect one's ability to spend a particular amount of money on a home.

Consider this advice in the lending area of the site: "When you don't have the cash on hand for important purchases, we can help you borrow what you need. From a new car to that vacation you've been longing for, to new kitchen appliances, you can make these dreams real now." Click on a button at the bottom of this screen — and presto, you're on your way to racking up credit card and auto debt. Why bother practicing delayed gratification, living within your means, or buying something used if getting a loan is "easy" and comes with "special privileges"?

Watching out for "sponsored" content

Sponsored content, a euphemism for advertising under the guise of editorial content (known in the print media as *advertorials*), is another big problem to watch out for on websites. You may find a disclaimer or note, which is often buried in small print in an obscure part of the website, saying that an article is sponsored by (in other words, paid advertising by) the "author."

A mutual-fund "education" site, for example, states that its "primary purpose is to provide viewers with an independent guide that contains information and articles they can't get anywhere else." The content of the site suggests otherwise. In the "Expert's Corner" section of the site, material is reprinted from a newsletter that advocates frequent trading in and out of mutual funds to try and guess and time market moves. Turns out that the article is "sponsored by the featured expert": In other words, it's a paid advertisement. (The track record of the newsletter's past recommendations, which isn't discussed on the site, is poor.)

WARNING

Even more troubling are the many websites that fail to disclose (even cryptically) that their "content" comes from advertisers, and those that do often do so in far too small print buried at the bottom of a web page. Mind you, I'm not saying that disclosure makes paid-for content okay — I'm simply stating that a lack of disclosure makes an already bad situation even worse.

Also, beware of websites, especially those that are "free," that are making money in a clandestine way from two sources: companies whose products they praise and affiliates to whom they direct mouse clicks/web traffic. In perusing the web, I noticed, for example, that many "free" financial websites were singing the praises of some budgeting software. I test-drove the product (which is like a slimmed-down version of Quicken), and it was a decent but not exceptional product. My research uncovered the fact that the makers of this software paid a whopping 35-percent commission to website affiliates who pitched and directed users to buy the product. With the software selling for $60, a website flogging it for them pockets $21 for each copy it sells. Does that taint a site's recommendation of the software? Of course it does.

Increasingly, companies are paying websites outright to simply mention and praise their products; doing so is incredibly sleazy even if it's disclosed, but to do so without disclosure is unethical. Also, beware of links to recommended product and service providers to do business with — more often than not, the referring website gets paid an affiliate fee. Look for sites that post policies against receiving such referral fees from companies whose products and services they recommend. (As an example, see the disclosure I use on my own site, www.erictyson.com.)

Steering clear of biased financial-planning advice

I also suggest skipping the financial-planning advice offered by financial service companies that are out to sell you something. Such companies can't take the necessary objective, holistic view required to render useful advice.

For example, on one major investment company's website, you find a good deal of material on the firm's mutual funds. The site's college-planning advice is off the mark because it urges parents to put money in a custodial account in the child's name. Ignored is the fact that doing so will undermine your child's ability to qualify for financial aid, that your child will have control of the money at either age 18 or 21 depending upon your state, and that you're likely better off funding your employer's retirement plan. If you did that, though, you couldn't set up a college savings-plan account at the investment company.

Shunning short-term thinking

WARNING

Many financial websites provide real-time stock quotes as a hook to a site that is cluttered with advertising. My experience working with individual investors is that the more short-term they think, the worse they do. And checking your portfolio during the trading day certainly promotes short-term thinking.

Another way that sites create an addictive environment for you to return to multiple times daily is to constantly provide news and other rapidly changing content. Do you really need "Breaking News" updates that gasoline prices jumped 19 cents per gallon over the past two weeks or that yet another social media personality is having a contest with a Hollywood celebrity to see who can sign up more X (formerly Twitter) followers in the next week?

Also, beware of tips offered around the electronic water cooler — comment sections. As in the real world, chatting with strangers and exchanging ideas are sometimes fine. However, if you don't know the identity and competence of commenters, why would you follow their financial advice or stock tips? Getting ideas from various sources is okay, but educate yourself and do your homework before making personal financial decisions.

TIP

If you want to best manage your personal finances and find out more, remember that the old expression "You get what you pay for" contains a grain of truth. Free information on the internet, especially information provided by companies in the financial services industry, is largely self-serving. Stick with information providers who have proven themselves offline or who don't have anything to sell except objective information and advice.

Checking out blogs, podcasts, and newsletters

While there have long been printed investment newsletters, the rise of the internet has produced an explosion of blogs, podcasts, and online newsletters about money. The biggest problem with this is that there are virtually no barriers to entry, especially and most importantly in terms of qualifications, knowledge, and experience.

Far too many of these outfits have major conflicts of interest and agendas. If you're considering reading or listening to any online personal finance outlet, first thoroughly check out the background and expertise of the people behind the endeavor. And investigate how they are making money and what they are pushing. If these things are hidden or sketchy, run away!

TIP

I also find it helpful to listen to and read episodes and articles from years past to see how that advice turned out for those who followed it.

Navigating newspapers and magazines

Compared with radio and TV, print publications (many of which have migrated online) generally offer lengthier discussions of topics. And in the more financially focused publications, the editors who work on articles generally have more background in the topics they write about. Even within the better publications, I find a wide variety of quality. So don't instantly believe what you read, even if you read a piece in a publication you like. Here's how to get the most from financial publications:

>> **Read some back issues.** Go to your local library (or visit the publication's website) and peruse some issues that are at least one to two years old. Although reading old issues may seem silly and pointless, it actually can be enlightening. You can begin to get a taste of a publication's style, priorities, and philosophies as well as how its prior advice has worked out.

>> **Look for solid information and perspective.** Headlines reveal a lot about how a publication perceives its role. Publications with cover stories such as "10 hot stocks to buy now!" and "Funds that will double your money in the next three years!" are probably best avoided. Look for articles that seek to educate with accuracy, not make predictions.

>> **Note bylines.** As you read a given publication over time, you should begin to make note of the different writers. After you get to know who the better writers are, you can skip over the ones you don't care for and spend your limited free time reading the best.

>> **Don't react without planning.** Here's a common example of how *not* to use information and advice that you glean from publications: I had a client who had some cash he wanted to invest. He would read an article about investing in real-estate investment trusts and then go out the next week and buy several of them. Then he'd see a mention of some technology stock funds and invest in some of those. Eventually, his portfolio was a mess of investments that reflected the history of what he had read rather than an orchestrated, well-thought-out investment portfolio.

Betting on books

Reading a good book is one of my favorite ways to get a crash course on a given financial topic. Good books can go into depth on a topic in a way that simply isn't possible with other resources. Books also aren't cluttered with advertising and the conflicts inherent therein.

As with the other types of resources that I discuss in this chapter, you definitely have to choose carefully — plenty of mediocrity and garbage is out there. Authors write books for many reasons other than to teach and educate. The most common reason financial book authors write books is to further their own business interests. If an author is using a book simply to market their services as a financial advisor, for example, that's not the best thing for you when you're trying to educate yourself and better manage your own finances.

Here's a list of some of my favorite financial titles (please also see the book summaries I provide on my website, www.erictyson.com):

>> *A Random Walk Down Wall Street* by Burton G. Malkiel (Norton)

>> *Built to Last: Successful Habits of Visionary Companies* by Jim Collins and Jerry I. Porras (HarperCollins)

>> *Good to Great: Why Some Companies Make the Leap . . . and Others Don't* by Jim Collins (HarperCollins)

>> Nolo's legal titles

>> And not surprisingly, my *For Dummies* books on investing, mutual funds, home buying, house selling, mortgages, real-estate investing, small business, and paying for college (all published by Wiley)

Observing the Mass Media

For better and for worse, America's mass media, including social media, has a major influence on our culture. On the good side, news is widely disseminated these days. So if a product is recalled or a dangerous virus breaks out in your area, you'll probably hear about it, perhaps more than you want to, through the media or from tuned-in family members! The downsides of the mass media and social media are plenty, though.

Alarming or informing?

The media loves a good crisis. During the "financial crisis" of 2008–2009, we heard over and over and over again how it was the worst economy and worst economic crisis since the Great Depression. Endless parallels were drawn between the Great Depression of the 1930s and the then slumping economy.

For sure, we suffered a significant recession (economic downturn). But some in the news media (and pundit class) went overboard in suggesting we were in the midst of another depression. During the Great Depression of the 1930s, the unemployment rate hit 25 percent and remained in double digits for years on end. Half of all homes ended up in foreclosure during that period. Although job losses and home foreclosures mounted during the 2008–2009 recession, they were nowhere near the Great Depression levels. The recessions of the late 1970s and early 1980s were actually worse because of the pain and hardship caused by the 10+ percent inflation rate and interest rates of that period. The unemployment rate was also above 10 percent in the early 1980s recession.

The U.S. stock market suffered a steep decline during the 2008 financial crisis and recession, and in fact, the percentage decline in the widely followed Dow Jones Industrial Average was the worst since the 1930s. Interestingly, the severity of the 2008–2009 stock market decline was likely exacerbated by all the talk and fear of another depression. Various research polls taken during late 2008 found that more than six in ten Americans believed we were about to enter another Great Depression. Those who panicked and bailed out when the Dow sagged below 6,500 in early 2009 learned another hard lesson when the market surged back, as it always inevitably does after a significant sell-off. (To date, the Dow has approximately risen more than five-fold in value since that market bottom in 2009).

WARNING

Some news producers, in their quest for ratings and advertising dollars, try to be alarming to keep you tuned in and coming back for their "breaking news" updates. The more you watch, the more unnerved you get over short-term, especially negative, events.

Teaching questionable values

Daily doses of American mass media and social media, including all the advertising that comes with them, essentially communicate the following messages:

>> Your worth as a person is directly related to your physical appearance (including the quality of clothing and jewelry you wear) and your material possessions — cars, homes, electronics, and other gadgets.

>> The more money you make, the more "successful" you clearly are.

- The more famous you are (especially as a movie or sports star), the more you're worth listening to and admiring.

- Don't bother concerning yourself with the consequences before engaging in negative behavior.

- Delaying gratification and making sacrifices are for boring losers.

WARNING

Continually inundating yourself with poor messages can cause you to behave in a way that undermines your long-term happiness and financial success. Don't support (by watching, listening to, or reading) forms of media that don't reflect your values and morals.

Worshiping prognosticating pundits

Quoting and interviewing "experts" are perhaps the only things that the media loves more than hyping short-term news events. What's the economy going to do next quarter? Which stocks will rise and which will fall next month? What's the stock market going to do in the next few hours? No, I'm not kidding about that last one — the stock market cable channel CNBC interviews floor traders from the New York Stock Exchange during the trading day to get their opinions about what the market will do in the hours just before closing!

WARNING

Prognosticating pundits keep many people tuned in because their advice is constantly changing (and is therefore entertaining and anxiety-producing), and they lead investors to believe that investments can be maneuvered in advance to outfox future financial market moves. Common sense suggests, though, that no one has a working crystal ball, and if they did, they certainly wouldn't share such insights with the mass media for free.

Navigating social media

In recent decades, social media platforms like Facebook, Instagram, Pinterest, Reddit, TikTok, X (formerly Twitter), and YouTube have roared onto the scene. Fans of some of these platforms point to the interactivity, timeliness, and wide range of content as attractions. Critics point to addictiveness, lack of editorial oversight, and biases as drawbacks.

WARNING

Social media platforms and blogs have been a tremendous source of misleading hype and outright fraud. For example, scores of self-anointed stock-picking gurus claim ridiculously hyped and bogus returns, and unfortunately, many of them evade regulatory scrutiny or punishment. I've been quite disappointed by the large volume of obvious hype online, especially on social media platforms.

Here are some commonalities I've observed over time among stock-picking touts online that you should sidestep and avoid:

>> They rarely or never post their suggested stock trades in advance. They tell you after the fact about stocks they claim to have previously bought.

>> They report their own calculated super high returns and don't have an outside or independent audit to substantiate their high and inflated claims.

>> They delete postings that make them look bad.

A lot of money is sloshing around out there, and there are so many venues and ways in which hucksters and criminals will try to separate you from your money. Simply put, you should always be extremely careful listening to any advice or recommendations, especially when they're coming from a source you don't know well in terms of their expertise, conflicts of interest, and what they are implicitly or explicitly seeking to sell you.

Chapter **11**

Ten Ways to Prevent Identity Theft and Fraud

Hucksters and thieves are often several steps ahead of law enforcement. Eventually, some of the bad guys get caught, but many don't, and those who do get nabbed often go back to their unsavory ways after penalties and some jail time.

Please follow the ten tips in this chapter to keep yourself from falling prey and unnecessarily losing money.

Save Phone Discussions for Friends Only

WARNING

Never, ever give out personal information over the phone, especially when you aren't the one who initiated the call. Suppose you get a call and the person on the other end of the line claims to be with a company you conduct business with (such as your credit card company or bank). Ask for the caller's name and number and call back the company's main number (which you look up) to be sure the person who called you is indeed with that company and has a legitimate business reason for contacting you.

With caller ID on your phone line, you may be able to see what number a call is originating from, but often calls from business-registered phone numbers come up as "unavailable." And crooks have gotten more advanced and can "spoof" real phone numbers that aren't actually the numbers they are calling from. A major red flag: calling back the number that comes through on caller ID and discovering that the number is bogus (a nonworking number).

Never Respond to Emails Soliciting Information

You may have seen or heard about official-looking emails sent from companies you know of and may do business with asking you to promptly visit their website to correct some sort of billing or account problem. Crooks can generate a return/sender email address that looks like it comes from a known institution but really does not. This unscrupulous practice is known as *phishing*, and if you bite at the bait, visit the site, and provide the requested personal information, your reward is likely to be some sort of future identity-theft problem and possibly a computer virus.

To find out more about how to protect yourself from phishing scams, visit the website of the Anti-Phishing Working Group (APWG) at apwg.org/.

Review Your Monthly Financial Statements

Although financial institutions such as banks may call you if they notice unusual activity on one of your accounts, some people discover problematic account activity by simply reviewing their monthly credit card, checking account, and other statements.

Do you need to balance bank account statements to the penny? No, you don't. I haven't for years (decades actually), and I don't have the time or patience for such minutiae. The key is to review the line items on your statement to be sure that all the transactions were yours and are correct.

Secure All Receipts

When you make a purchase, be sure to keep track of and secure receipts, especially those that contain your personal financial or account information. You can keep these in an envelope in your home, for example. Then cross-check them against your monthly statement.

REMEMBER

When you no longer need to retain your receipts, be sure to dispose of them in a way that prevents a thief, who may get into your garbage, from being able to decipher the information on them. Rip up the receipts or, if you feel so inclined, buy a small paper shredder for your home and/or small business.

Close Unnecessary Credit Accounts

Open your wallet and remove all the pieces of plastic within it that enable you to charge purchases. The more credit cards and credit lines you have, the more likely you are to have problems with identity theft and fraud and the more likely you are to overspend and carry debt balances. Also, reduce preapproved credit offers by contacting 888-5OPTOUT (888-567-8688) or visiting www. optoutprescreen.com.

Unless you maintain a card for small-business transactions, you really "need" only one piece of plastic with a Visa or Mastercard logo. Give preference to a debit card or other direct payment methods if you have a history of accumulating credit card debt.

Regularly Review Your Credit Reports

You may be tipped off to shenanigans going on in your name when you review your credit report. Some identity-theft victims have found out about credit accounts opened in their name by reviewing their credit reports.

TIP

Because you're entitled to a free credit report from each of the three major credit agencies every year, I recommend reviewing your reports at least that often. The reports generally contain the same information, so you can request and review one agency report every four months, which enables you to keep a closer eye on your reports and still obtain them without cost. (Be sure to use the free site www.annualcreditreport.com.)

I don't generally recommend spending the $100 or so annually for a so-called credit monitoring service that updates you when something happens on your credit reports. If you're concerned about someone illegally applying for credit in your name, know that another option for you to stay on top of things is to "freeze" your personal credit reports and scores (see the next section).

Freeze Your Credit Reports or Place an Alert

To address the growing problem of identity theft, all states have credit freeze laws, which enable consumers to prevent access to their personal credit reports. And the law requires that you can freeze your credit file for free.

In some states, only identity-theft victims may freeze their reports. The individual whose credit report is frozen is the only person who may grant access to the frozen credit report.

A fraud alert requires creditors to verify your identity before processing credit applications. If you suspect that you've been a victim of identity theft, you can place an initial fraud report for one year. Active-duty service members can also place a one-year alert to protect their credit file. An extended fraud alert can be placed for seven years if you file an identity theft report with the police or Federal Trade Commission (FTC). Alerts also remove you from prescreened credit and insurance offers.

Credit freezes and fraud alerts are designed to prevent identity thieves from opening loans or credit accounts in your name.

Keep Personal Info Off Your Checks

Don't place personal information on checks. Information that is useful to identity thieves — and that you should not put on your checks — includes your credit card number, driver's license number, Social Security number, and so on. I also encourage you to leave your home address off your preprinted checks when you order them. Otherwise, every Tom, Dick, and Jane whose hands your check passes through knows exactly where you live.

When writing a check to a merchant, question the need for adding personal information to the check (in fact, in numerous states, requesting and placing credit card numbers on checks is against the law). Remember that your credit card doesn't advertise your home address and other financial account data, so there's no need to publicize it to the world on your checks.

Protect Your Computer and Files

Especially if you keep personal and financial data on your computer, consider the following safeguards to protect your computer and the confidential information on it:

>> Install a firewall.

>> Use virus protection software.

>> Password-protect access to your programs and files.

Safeguard Your Mail

Some identity thieves have collected personal information by simply helping themselves to mail in home mailboxes. Stealing mail is easy, especially if your mail is delivered to a curbside box.

Consider using a locked mailbox or a post office box to protect your incoming mail from theft. Consider having your investment and other important statements sent to you via email, or simply access them online and eliminate mail delivery of paper copies.

Check washing, the process of erasing details on checks and rewriting them, is a common fraud involving stolen mail containing checks. Amazon and office supply stores sell fraud prevention writing pens with ink that can't be washed.

REMEMBER

Be careful with your outgoing mail as well, such as bills with checks attached. Minimize your outgoing mail and save yourself hassles by signing up for automatic bill payment for as many bills as possible. Drop the rest of your outgoing mail in a secure U.S. postal box, such as those you find at the local post office.

Index

A

AccuQuote, 64

adaptability, as financial chameleon's superpower, 129–142

advanced directives, 120–124

advanced healthcare directive, 124

advertorials, cautions with, 146

Aetna, 55

Affordable Care Act (ACA) (2010), 18, 52–56, 135

agent (in POA), 118

Aging with Dignity, Five Wishes, 124

allocations
  for long term, 96–97
  sticking with, 98

American Rescue Plan Act (ARP) (2021), 18

annuities, 82–83

Anthem, 55

Anti-Phishing Working Group (APWG), 156

"Application for a Social Security Card" (Form SS-5), 77

appreciation, of stocks, 88

asset allocation, 96

assets
  allocation of, 96
  buying LTC insurance to retain and protect assets, 58
  cautions against signing over checks and security certificates to financial advisor, 84
  estate planning for determining what will happen to yours, 113–115
  management of through POA, 118, 119
  shielding yours from unexpected twists, 64–68

assistance, finding assistance from family, 16–17

Assurant, 55

attorney-in-fact (in POA), 118

auto insurance, 64, 66–68

autos
  cautions with loaning or leasing of, 44
  reduction in spending on, 44

B

bad debt, defined, 30

bankruptcy
  benefits of, 37
  Chapter 7, 39, 40–41
  Chapter 13, 40–41
  deciphering laws of, 39
  drawbacks of, 38–39
  filing for, 37–41

Bankruptcy Abuse and Prevention Act (2005), 39

bear markets, 28–29

beneficiaries

passing money to without having to pay federal estate taxes, 116–117

reconsideration of when marrying, 134

as reflecting your current wishes, 114

special-needs beneficiaries, 115

bias

recognizing of regarding financial information, 145

steering clear of biased financial-planning advice, 147

blogs, choosing them carefully for your financial education, 148

Blue Cross, Blue Shield, 55

boneheaded financial actions, avoidance of, 29–30

books, choosing them carefully for your financial education, 149–150

brokerage firms, use of, 85, 93

budget, setting and following of, 46–49

Built to Last: Successful Habits of Visionary Companies (Collins and Porras), 150

business, preparing for financial success when starting a small business, 137

bypass trust, 117

C

capital gains

consideration of, 72–73

defined, 72, 88

long-term capital gains, 72–73, 88, 105

short-term capital gains, 73

cars. *See* autos

cash sources, for using savings to reduce consumer debt, 31–33

cash value life insurance, 9, 15, 31–32, 62–63, 117

Center for Poverty and Inequality Research (U.C. Davis), 19

changing circumstances, making money decisions amid, 10

Chapter 7 bankruptcy, 39, 40–41

Chapter 13 bankruptcy, 40–41

charitable contributions, analysis of spending on, 46

check washing, 159

checks, keeping personal information off yours, 158–159

Child Tax Credit (CTC), 19

childcare

analysis of spending on, 46

tax benefits of, 136

children

avoiding indulgence of, 137

preparing for financial success when having children, 134–135

taxing issues regarding, 77

Children's Health Insurance Program (CHIP), 56

CIGNA, 55

clothing, reduction in spending on, 45

Collins, Jim, 150

compatibility test, for couples preparing for marriage, 132

compound interest,
magic of, 79–87

computer, protection of
regarding personal and
financial data, 159

consumer credit, 106

consumer debt

bad debt vs. good debt, 30

battling of, 31–49

impact of on financial goals, 106

using savings to reduce, 31–33

Consumer Reports, 44, 48

credit cards

applying for lower-rate one, 33

cancelling high-interest
ones, 33–34

closing unnecessary ones, 157

as compared with debit cards, 35

cutting up yours, 34

paying off consumer
loans on, 32–33

responsible use of, 130

secured credit card, 38

Credit Counseling & Debtor
Education (U.S. Trustee), 39

credit counseling agencies, 35–37

credit monitoring service, 158

credit reports

freezing yours or placing an
alert, 158

reviewing yours, 157–158

creditors, defined, 38

crises. See economic crises/
hardships/ups and downs;
financial crises; major crises;
medical crises; personal crises

CTC (Child Tax Credit), 19

custodial accounts,
cautions with, 136

D

Database of State Incentives for
Renewables & Efficiency, 45

DCA (dollar-cost averaging),
investing lump sums
via, 98–99

death

beneficiaries. See beneficiaries

of spouse, tapping resources
after, 24–25

debit cards

as compared with
credit cards, 35

defined, 34–35

debt

avoiding new debt, 41–49

decreasing of when you lack
savings, 33–41

managing feelings about, 27–30

paying off high-interest
debt, 30–41

reducing and repaying of,
27–49

wise financial actions to take
regarding, 29

debt management programs
(DMPs), 36

debtor education, 39

decision making

avoiding boneheaded financial
actions, 29–30

taking time for, 13

declaration (auto insurance
statement), 66

deductions, strengthening yours, 73–74

dependent care tax credit, 77

direct trustee-to-trustee transfer, 83

disabilities, insurance coverage for, 58–61

discretionary spending, reduction of, 29

diversification

in asset allocation, 96

benefits of, 95

as powerful investment concept, 92, 95–99

dividends, from stocks, 87

divorce

regaining financial stability after, 29

tapping resources during and after, 23–24

DMPs (debt management programs), 36

do not hospitalize (DNH) order, 122, 123

do not resuscitate (DNR) order, 122, 123

dollar-cost averaging (DCA), investing lump sums via, 98–99

Dow Jones Industrial Average, 151

durable power of attorney, 119

E

Earned Income Tax Credit (EITC), 19

economic crises/hardships/ups and downs. See also financial crises

adopting positive mindset during, 129

making money decisions amid, 10

riding them, 125–129

Edmunds, 44

education

continuing your financial education, 143–153

importance of continuing your general education, 131

elder care, tapping resources when caring for elderly parents unexpectedly, 21–22

emails, cautions with responding to emails soliciting information, 156

emergency reserves

accessing of, 15

building of, 12–13, 47–48

emotions

management of emotional upheavals, 12

management of in times of economic hardship, 129

managing feelings about debt, 27–30

employee benefits, review of, 7, 12–13

employer's retirement account, borrowing against yours, 32

employment

being prepared for job changes, 131–132

preparing for financial success when starting out at your first job, 130

tapping resources after job loss, 20–21

employment income taxes, trimming of, 74–77

entertainment, reduction in spending on, 44–45

estate planning
advanced directives, 120–124
defined, 113
with elderly parents, 22
power of attorney (POA), 117–120
reducing estate taxes, 116–117
signing DNRs, 122–123
trusts, 115, 117
wills, 114, 116, 133, 136

estate taxes, reduction of, 116–117

exchange-traded funds (ETFs)
buying stocks via, 88–90
as diversified portfolios, 95
as good choices for IRA investments, 82
as part of investment portfolio, 87

expenditures
going easy on everyday ones, 111–112
reduction of, 41–46

F

Facebook, 152

family
children. *See* childcare; children
divorce. *See* divorce
finding assistance from, 16–17, 32
marriage. *See* marriage; spouse

Federal Deposit Insurance Corporation (FDIC), 126

Federal Housing Assistance programs (HUD), 19

federal income tax brackets and rates, 70

Federal Reserve, 126

Federal Trade Commission, 36

files, protection of regarding personal and financial data, 159

financial crises
making money decisions amid, 10
of 1907, 126
of 2008, 125, 126, 150

financial education, continuing yours, 143–153

financial goals
dealing with competing ones, 105–106
knowing what's most important to you, 103–106
saving for big purchases, 106
setting of, 101–112

financial health, assessing current personal financial health, 6–7

financial independence, dreaming of, 101–103

Financial Industry Regulatory Authority (FINRA), 86

financial information, identifying reliable sources of, 143–153

financial lingo, grasping of, 7–8

financial plan, elements of, 6–7

financial power of attorney, 117

financial publications, getting the most from, 148–149

financial resilience, in volatile world, 125–142

financial safety net
establishment of, 11–26
inventorying your resources, 15–19
knowing when to tap your resources, 20–26
preparing for unplanned events, 11–14

financial security
assessing current personal financial health, 6–7
dealing with insurance, 9–10
defining what you value, 4–6
grasping financial lingo and trends, 7–8
making decisions about money amid changing circumstances, 10
trying not to avoid money, 8–9

Financial Security For Dummies (Tyson), 126

financial stability, knowing how long it will take to regain, 28–29

financial statements, reviewing yours, 156

financial strategies, that work, 128–129

financial trends, grasping of, 7–8

financial windfall, tips to make most of, 138–139

Five Wishes (Aging with Dignity), 124

flexibility, importance of, 13

flexible benefit plans, 22

food and dining, reduction in spending on, 43–44

For Dummies books, 150

401(k) accounts, 71, 75, 81, 83

403(b) accounts, 71, 75, 81, 83

fraud, prevention of, 155–160

G

gifting
allowances for tax-free gifting, 116–117
buying more for people you love, 111

good debt, defined, 30

Good to Great: Why Some Companies Make the Leap . . . and Others Don't (Collins), 150

Goodwill, 45

gratification, learning to delay or modify, 106

Great Depression, 150, 151

H

Health Care and Education Reconciliation Act, 52

health insurance. *See also specific plans*
buying of, 54–55
choosing a plan, 53
co-payments, 54
deductibles, 54
employer-provided coverage, 51, 52
guaranteed renewability, 54
lifetime maximum benefits, 54
major medical coverage, 53
subsidies, 18–19, 55–56

health insurance exchange, 55

Health Insurance Portability and Accountability Act (HIPPA) (1996), authorizing of, 123

health maintenance organizations (HMOs), 53, 54

healthcare power of attorney, 123

healthcare proxy, 121–122, 123

hedge funds, 87, 90

high-interest debt, paying it off, 30–41

home
  assessment of, 7
  preparing to buy one, 134
  reduction of housing expenses, 42
  renting vs. ownership, 42–43
  taking equity out of to reduce consumer debt, 32

homeowner's insurance, 64, 65–66

housing, help with, 19

Housing and Urban Development (HUD), Federal Housing Assistance programs, 19

Housing Choice Voucher Program (Section 8 or Tenant Based Rental Assistance), 19

I

icons, explained, 2

identity theft, prevention of, 155–160

income
  shifting of, 76–77
  structuring finances to afford dip in, 131–132
  tapping resources after loss of, 20–21

income taxes
  knowing your rate, 69–70
  making your income tax rate work for you, 71–74
  quarterly tax filing requirements, 78
  taxing issues regarding children, 76–77
  trimming employment income taxes, 74–77

individual retirement accounts (IRAs), 81–82, 86. See also 401(k) accounts; 403(b) accounts; SEP-IRA (Simplified Employee Pension-Individual Retirement) accounts

Instagram, 152

Institute for Financial Literacy, 36

insurance. See also health insurance; life insurance; long-term care (LTC) insurance; long-term disability (LTD) insurance; renter's insurance; umbrella insurance
  avoiding overspending on, 45–46
  dealing with, 9–10
  ensuring adequate coverage, 17–18
  importance of, 130–131
  as protection, 51–68
  review of, 7

investing
  getting in habit of, 130
  getting smart about, 110
  for the long haul, 79–87
  of lump sums via dollar-cost averaging, 98–99
  proven strategies for, 92–93

Investing For Dummies (Tyson), 92, 97

investment portfolio
assessment of, 7
choosing investments wisely, 72

IRS Form 940, 78

IRS Form 941, 78

IRS Form 1040-ES, 78

IRS Form 2441 (dependent care tax credit), 77

IRS Form 5695, 45

J

jobs. *See* employment

K

Kaiser Permanente, 55

Kelley Blue Book, 44

L

life changes, preparing for, 11–14

life insurance
borrowing against cash value of, 31–32
cash value life insurance, 9, 31, 62–63, 117
figuring out how much you need, 63–64
need for, 61
tapping cash value balances, 15
term life insurance, 62–63

living trusts, 115

living wills, 121–122

loans
cautions with auto loans, 44

paying off consumer loans on credit cards, 32–33
taking out, 15

long-term capital gains, 72–73, 88, 105

long-term care (LTC) insurance, 57–58

long-term disability (LTD) insurance, 57–61

luxury spending, avoiding new debt with, 41

M

magazines, choosing them carefully for your financial education, 148–149

mail
cautions with responding to emails soliciting information, 156
safeguarding your snail mail, 159–160

major crises, riding ups and downs during, 125–129

major medical coverage, 53

Malkiel, Burton G., 150

marginal income tax rate, 70, 71

marriage. *See also* divorce
preparing to make financial decisions when marrying, 132–134
tapping resources after marriage split up, 23–24

mass media, observation of regarding financial information, 150–153

maternity leave, 136

Means Testing Information (U.S. Trustee), 40

mediation, divorce by
    mediation, 24
Medicaid
  defined, 18
  healthcare subsidies and, 56
medical care directive, 120–121
medical crises, tapping resources
    during, 21
Medicare
  closing gaps in, 56–57
  defined, 18, 51, 56
  healthcare subsidies and, 56
  maximizing benefits from, 56–58
  Medicare tax rates, 52
  Part A (hospital expenses), 56
  Part B (physical expenses and
      other charges), 56
  Part C (supplemental), 56
  Part D (prescription drugs),
      56, 57, 58
Medigap, 56
mega-liability, umbrella insurance
    as protecting against, 68
mental health, taking time for, 13
misinformation, avoiding
    heeding misinformation and
    uninformed people on social
    media platforms and blogs, 127
mistakes, avoiding common
    ones, 127–128
money
  allocating of for long term, 96–97
  getting smart about investing
    yours, 110
  hoarding of, 107, 111
  keeping accumulation of in
    proper perspective, 109
  making decisions about amid
    changing circumstances, 10

reducing time spent on earning
    and spending of, 49
safety of during financial
    crises, 126
trying not to avoid it,
    8–9
mutual funds
  buying stocks via,
    88–90
  as diversified portfolios, 95
  as good choices for IRA
    investments, 82

N

natural disaster, dealing
    with, 25–26
needs vs. wants, 48
net worth, analysis of, 6
news (media)
  as alarming or
    informing? 150–151
  avoiding immersing yourself in
    excessive and negative
    short-term news, 128
  news diet, 110, 128
newsletters, choosing them
    carefully for your financial
    education, 148
newspapers, choosing them
    carefully for your financial
    education, 148–149
Nolo, 116, 150

O

Obamacare, 18, 52. *See also*
    Affordable Care Act
    (ACA) (2010)
100-percent joint and survivor
    option, 141

open mindedness, importance of, 13

over-saving, 107–112

overspending, 108–109

P

Patient Protection and Affordable Care Act (2010), 52. *See also* Affordable Care Act (ACA) (2010)

penny stocks, cautions with, 94

pension options, 141–142

personal crises, navigation of, 13–14

Personal Finance For Dummies (Tyson), 23

personal financial plan, 6–7

personal information
  cautions with giving it out over phone, 155–156
  keeping it off your checks, 158–159
  protecting your computer and files, 159

PHAs (Public Housing Agencies), 19

phishing, 156

Pinterest, 152

podcasts, choosing them carefully for your financial education, 148

politicians, avoiding listening to, 128

Porras, Jerry I., 150

positive mindset, adopting of during times of economic hardship, 129

power of attorney (POA)
  choosing the right one, 119–120

durable power of attorney, 119

financial power of attorney, 117

healthcare power of attorney, 123

importance of, 118

springing power of attorney, 119

predictions, avoiding following, prognosticators who claim to have predicted bad things, 127

preferred provider organizations (PPOs), 53

prescription drug program (Medicare), 58

privately managed funds, use of, 90

probate
  avoidance of, 115
  defined, 115

procrastination, cautions with, 8, 12, 129

products, looking for best values for, 49

Public Housing Agencies (PHAs), 19

pundits, cautions with worshipping them, 152

purchases, saving for big ones, 106

R

A Random Walk Down Wall Street (Malkiel), 150

receipts, securing them, 157

recreation, reduction in spending on, 44–45

Reddit, 152

ReliaQuote, 64

relocating, evaluating total financial picture when relocating, 132

renter's insurance, 65

renting vs. ownership of home, 42–43

research
  importance of doing before making decisions, 13
  valuing of, 48

Residential Energy Credits, 45

resources
  knowing when to tap yours, 20–26
  taking inventory of, 15–19

retirement
  analysis in planning for, 109–110
  maintaining standard of living in, 102–103
  tips to help you through, 140–142

retirement account, defined, 80

retirement funds/accounts
  borrowing from, 16, 32
  causes of lack of, 9
  choices of, 80–83
  company-based plans, 81
  compound interest and, 79–99
  contributions to, 43, 71–72, 74–76
  early withdrawal penalties, 106
  individual retirement accounts (IRAs), 81–82, 86
  tax advantages of, 82–83, 92–93, 104–105
  transferring of, 83–87
  valuing of, 104–106

retirement investment plan, 74–76

Roth 401(k) accounts, 81

Roth IRA, 82

S

safety nets
  finding out about, 13
  qualifying for societal safety nets, 18–19

Salvation Army, 45

Saver's Credit, 75–76

savings
  analysis of, 6
  avoiding over-saving, 107–112
  balancing of with spending, 108–109
  boosting of by reducing spending, 48
  decreasing debt when you lack savings, 33
  making it a habit, 49, 130

SBA (Small Business Administration), 138

SBDC (Small Business Development Centers), 138

Schedule C (Profit or Loss from Business), 74

Section 8 (Housing Choice Voucher Program), 19

Securities and Exchange Commission (SEC), 86

self-employment, retirement plans for, 81

SEP-IRA (Simplified Employee Pension-Individual Retirement) accounts, 71, 75, 81, 82, 83

Serenity Prayer, 28

short-term capital gains, 73

short-term thinking, cautions with, 147–148

Small Business Administration (SBA), 138

Small Business Development Centers (SBDC), 138

Small Business Taxes For Dummies (Tyson), 74

snail mail, safeguarding yours, 159–160

social media, navigation of, 152–153

Social Security Administration (SSA)

"Application for a Social Security Card" (Form SS-5), 77

contacting, 8–9

Social Security Disability Insurance program, 59, 60

spending

analysis of, 6

balancing of with saving, 108–109

boosting savings by reducing, 48

buying more gifts for people you love, 111

giving yourself permission to spend more, 109

reduction of, 41–46

treating yourself to something special, 111

sponsored content, cautions with, 146

spouse. *See also* marriage

coping with death of, 24–25

tapping resources during and after divorce from, 23–24

springing power of attorney, 119

SSA (Social Security Administration). *See* Social Security Administration (SSA)

state disability insurance programs, 59–60

stocks

advantages of stock funds, 88–89

avoiding problematic buying practices, 93

avoiding selling stocks at greatly reduced/depressed prices, 127

buying of via mutual funds and exchange-traded funds, 88–90

cautions with penny stocks, 94

drawbacks of stock funds, 89–90

intended as long-term holdings, 87, 94

making money from, 87–94

selecting them yourself, 91–94

stress management, 12, 129

super savers, 107–108, 110

survivorship options, 141

T

T. Rowe Price, retirement tool, 110

tax advantages

of annuities, 82–83

of retirement accounts, 92–93, 104–105

tax consequences, understanding of, 13

tax credits

dependent care tax credit, 77

federal refundable tax credits, 19

Saver's Credit, 75–76

taxes
  income taxes. *See* income taxes
  lowering/reduction of, 43, 69–78
tax-sheltered annuities, 83
Tenant Based Rental Assistance (Housing Choice Voucher Program), 19
term life insurance, 62–63
TikTok, 152
tough times, preparing for, 12
transportation, reduction in spending on, 44
trusts
  bypass trust, 117
  living trust, 115

U

U.C. Davis, Center for Poverty and Inequality Research, 19
umbrella insurance, 68
unemployment insurance benefits, 18–19
UnitedHealth, 55
unplanned events, preparing for, 11–14
U.S. Trustee
  Credit Counseling & Debtor Education, 39
  Means Testing Information, 40
USAA, 64
utility bills, reduction in, 45

V

values
  defining what you value, 4–6
  mass media as teaching questionable ones, 151–152
Vanguard, retirement tool, 110

W

wants vs. needs, 48
wills
  preparation of, 116
  purpose of, 114
  updating of when having children, 136
  updating of when marrying, 133
work. *See* employment
work and consumption treadmill, consequences of being on, 49
worker's compensation, coverage with, 60

X

X (formerly Twitter), 152

Y

YouTube, 152

About the Authors

Eric Tyson, MBA, has been a personal financial writer, lecturer, and counselor for the past 25+ years. As his own boss, Eric has worked with and taught people from a myriad of income levels and backgrounds, so he knows the personal finance concerns and questions of real folks just like you.

After toiling away for too many years as a management consultant to behemoth financial-service firms, Eric decided to take his knowledge of the industry and commit himself to making personal financial management accessible to everyone. Despite being handicapped by a joint BS in Economics and Biology from Yale and an MBA from Stanford, Eric remains a master at "keeping it simple."

An accomplished freelance personal-finance writer, Eric is the author or coauthor of numerous other *For Dummies* national bestsellers on personal finance, investing, and home buying and is a syndicated columnist. His *Personal Finance For Dummies* won the Benjamin Franklin Award for Best Business Book.

Eric's work has been critically acclaimed in hundreds of publications and programs, including *Newsweek,* the *Los Angeles Times,* the *Chicago Tribune, Kiplinger's Personal Finance Magazine,* the *Wall Street Journal,* Bottom Line Personal, as well as NBC's *Today* show, ABC, CNBC, PBS's Nightly Business Report, CNN, FOX-TV, CBS national radio, Bloomberg Business Radio, and Business Radio Network. His website is www.erictyson.com.

Bob Carlson is editor of the monthly newsletter and website, *Retirement Watch.* Bob also is chairman of the board of trustees of the Fairfax County Employees' Retirement System, which has over $4 billion in assets. He has served on the board since 1992. He was a member of the board of trustees of the Virginia Retirement System, which oversaw $42 billion in assets, from 2001 to 2005.

His latest book is *Where's My Money: Secrets to Getting the Most Out of Your Social Security* (Regnery). His prior books include *Invest Like a Fox...Not Like a Hedgehog* and *The New Rules of Retirement,* both published by Wiley. He has written numerous other books and reports, including *Tax Wise Money Strategies* and *Retirement Tax Guide.* He also has been interviewed by or quoted in numerous publications, including the *Wall Street Journal, Reader's Digest, Barron's, AARP Bulletin, Money* magazine, *Worth* magazine, *Kiplinger's Personal Finance* magazine, the *Washington Post,* and many others. He has appeared on national television and on a number of radio programs. He is past editor of *Tax Wise Money.* The *Washington Post* calls Bob's advice "smart . . . savvy . . . sensible . . . valuable and imaginative."

Bob has been a guest on many local and nationally syndicated radio shows.

Bob received his JD and an MS (in accounting) from the University of Virginia, received his BS (in financial management) from Clemson University, and passed the CPA exam. He also is an instrument-rated private pilot.

Publisher's Acknowledgments

Executive Editor: Steve Hayes

Compilation Editor:
Colleen Diamond

Project Editor: Colleen Diamond

Copy Editor: Christine Pingleton

Production Editor:
Tamilmani Varadharaj

Senior Managing Editor:
Kristie Pyles

Cover Design and Image: Wiley